The Northwest Coastal Explorer

The Northwest Coastal Explorer

Your Guide to the Places, Plants, and Animals of the Pacific Coast

Robert Steelquist

Timber Press
Portland, Oregon

Frontispiece: Extreme Northwest. Cape Flattery is the northwesternmost point in the Lower 48 states.

Published in 2016 by Timber Press, Inc.
The Haseltine Building
133 S.W. Second Avenue, Suite 450
Portland, Oregon 97204-3527
timberpress.com

Printed in China

Text design by McGuire Barber Design
Cover design by Anna Eshelman

Library of Congress Cataloging-in-Publication Data

Names: Steelquist, Robert.
Title: The Northwest coastal explorer: your guide to the places, plants, and animals of the Pacific Coast / Robert Steelquist.
Description: Portland, Oregon: Timber Press, 2016. | Includes bibliographical references and index.
Identifiers: LCCN 2015047572 | ISBN 9781604696318 (paperback)
Subjects: LCSH: Natural history—Northwest, Pacific—Guidebooks. | Natural history—Pacific Coast (North America)—Guidebooks. | Coastal ecology—Northwest, Pacific—Guidebooks. | Coastal ecology—Pacific Coast (North America)—Guidebooks. | Natural areas—Northwest, Pacific—Guidebooks. | Natural areas—Pacific Coast (North America)—Guidebooks. | Northwest, Pacific—Guidebooks. | Pacific Coast (North America)—Guidebooks.
Classification: LCC QH104.5.N6 S74 2016 | DDC 508.795—dc23 LC record available at http://lccn.loc.gov/2015047572

A catalog record for this book is also available from the British Library.

Dedicated to the memory of
Jenny Ann Hall Steelquist, 1952–2013

Contents

Habitats of the Pacific Northwest Coast

**Coastal Forests
48**

**Rocky Shores
and Tide Pools
86**

**Sand Beaches
124**

Nearshore
162

Rivers
190

Estuaries
212

Preface

The challenge I have faced in working on this book has been to pack a geography spanning over nine degrees of Earth's latitude into a small book that introduces the natural history of one of Earth's most productive coasts—the Pacific Northwest. I chose to start with experiences—what I learned from exploring the coast from Vancouver Island to northern California, and how I've shared that knowledge with others as an interpretive naturalist, teacher, writer, parent, and friend.

For the moment, imagine we're on the coast now, about to hike into the forest on a trail that will wind along a steep slope as it descends to a remote beach. We can hear the surf faintly, feel the misty breeze, and smell the salty air, fragrant and cool. We'll encounter common things—the plants and animals that give the Pacific Northwest its particular natural character. We will see trees, shrubs, birds, and amphibians. Stepping onto the beach, our senses will be assaulted—the crash of waves, the vastness of the horizon, and encounters with things that have washed up, or that scurry away as we pass. At the far end, where the sand stops and rocks begin, we'll prowl tide pools, astonished at the variety of life forms that cling to the rocks or dart to hiding places in the water. This is the experience of exploring the coast. Of meeting its living residents and visitors, learning their connections to everything else and our connections to them.

Before we launch into our outdoor adventures, however, it is important to introduce the region as a whole and the forces that shape it. The introduction to this book touches on geology, climate, and the physical ocean processes that make marine life possible and so productive. It then addresses our roles as stewards of the environment—the coast and ocean in particular.

The book then introduces major habitat types: coastal forests, rocky shores and tide pools, sand beaches, nearshore, rivers, and estuaries.

Each section highlights common plants and animals that you will almost always see. Selecting these wasn't easy, as there are so many to choose from. But each species is important for many reasons. And each is connected, in so many ways, to many other species. They all represent threads in a complex tapestry—the magnificent cloth that we call life.

A getaway guide is also included as a general travel guide to areas where you can experience a variety of habitats in one trip—beaches and tide pools; forests and estuaries. Each region was chosen for its unique variations of natural features, habitats and experiences, learning opportunities, accessibility, and general proximity to the Northwest's population centers. Each getaway is offered as an inspiration—informed by my own lifetime of experience in the Pacific Northwest—that can provide a head start to your own research and travel planning.

Proper gear is essential. When we step into the forest, or hike to a beach, we are encountering nature in all its moods. Proper footwear and rain protection, sunglasses and sunscreen, drinking water and snacks—all are necessary. Having the right tools—binoculars, a magnifying glass, a small shovel for probing the sand—lets us see farther, look closer, or explore more thoroughly the world around us. In order to help you get properly equipped, comprehensive equipment lists are included in the safety and equipment section.

Learning from others will also enhance your experience in nature. Wherever they are offered, take advantage of guided naturalist walks, interpretive talks, and the publications and online resources of public agencies, nonprofit groups, and commercial guide services. These are the local experts, trained not just on plants and animals unique to their area, but also in ways to make learning fun, with hands-on activities and real-world examples.

Acknowledgments

The process of assembling and writing this book has given me the opportunity to see my own environment with fresh eyes. It has led me deep into my own experiences and knowledge, gained over a lifetime as a Northwest resident and over an entire career working as an outdoor educator and professional conservationist in organizations such as the National Park Service, Washington Department of Fish and Wildlife, and NOAA's Olympic Coast National Marine Sanctuary. It has rekindled in me the excitement of discovering our region's natural wonders. My journey would not have been successful or enjoyable without the help of many.

My sons, Peter and Daniel Steelquist, schooled me, early on, in ways to convey awe and respect for the environment as their parent, travel narrator, and family expedition leader. With their mother, my late wife Jenny, our family traced and retraced, many times, the journeys of discovery that would become this book. Grown men and adventurers on their own now, Peter and Daniel know the stories in this book by heart—figuratively and literally—just as they know the highways, towns, trails, and beaches of our Northwest homeland. Recalling our past family trips together made my return trips for research especially rewarding.

Scores of colleagues, throughout the years, contributed unknowingly to this book by sharing their knowledge and discoveries with me. In addition to a library of books and papers, I possess a library of memories of hikes, research cruises, field trips, and long conversations about marine resources and their conservation. Special thanks are due to Tom Gaskill and Glen Alexander, who introduced me to their haunts in South Slough and Padilla Bay estuaries. My former colleagues in NOAA's Office of National Marine Sanctuaries, too numerous to name individually, enriched my career, advanced my understanding, and inspired my commitment to the work of marine conservation.

I owe special thanks to the Makah Tribe and the Makah Cultural and Research Center for allowing me access to areas of Makah territory traditionally off limits to nontribal researchers and photographers. Specifically, Janine Ledford, a longtime colleague and friend, and director of the Makah Museum, led me to locations rich with Makah cultural meanings and helped me understand, in my limited way, their profound significance. Rebekah Monette, Dan Greene, and Ben Greene were very generous in providing boat access to marine waters within Makah territory for photography. Yurok Tribal members Bob McConnell and Rosie Clayburn helped me see the Yurok landscape in northern California as I had never seen it before. Likewise, Eirik Thorsgard and Briece Edwards of the Confederated Tribes of the Grand Ronde permitted me glimpses of Native perceptions of the Oregon Coast hidden to most. Exploring these coastal landscapes with such insight vastly enriched my experience.

Between the redwoods and Vancouver Island, dozens of unnamed professional naturalists answered my persistent questions and gave me advice, whether on whale-watch boats or coastal interpretive hikes. Their expertise and dedication to the resources and visitors they serve convince me that the profession of interpretation is in the hands of passionate and expert practitioners.

During my research, Katie Marks accompanied me on hikes to remote beaches and gave me constant encouragement through times when writing and photography challenges seemed overwhelming. Thank you, Katie, for your support and companionship. Bill and Jane Marks hosted me at their home at Iron Springs, Washington, during a crucial photography field trip.

Juree Sondker and Andrew Beckman of Timber Press saw the potential in this project and supported it from the beginning. Thoughtful editing by Michael Dempsey brought the disparate parts together into a unified whole. Sarah Milhollin, as able a photo editor as I have ever worked with, teased my best pictures out of a vast pile and offered advice that made later picture-taking better. Many photographers—Northwest nature lovers all—shared their pictures, products of their patience, and technical skills to bring these stories to life. It was a special privilege to work again with Tom and Pat Leeson, who helped me launch my writing career in 1984.

One of my greatest challenges was choosing those places, plants, and animals to include and, as a result, those to be omitted. With such richness to work with, these decisions were difficult. Selecting a few key species, a few important habitats, and a small sampling of important places to highlight in this book required judgments on my part that will seem arbitrary to some and just plain wrong to others. For those decisions, I take full responsibility. I encourage readers who want to experience more places and understand more of the natural legacy of our region to go beyond the limits of this book. Be coastal explorers.

Introduction

The Pacific Ocean is the dominant natural feature of the Pacific Northwest, influencing our maritime climate (12–14 feet of rain each year in the Hoh Rain Forest), the abundance of our forests (giant coast redwoods and Sitka spruce) and rivers (salmon), and forming one of the most productive marine ecosystems on the planet. The coastal regions of northern California, Oregon, Washington, and British Columbia are also population centers and engines of our economy. We know the ocean is important—after all, that's why our region is called the *Pacific* Northwest.

But what happens when we hear the sound of breaking surf through a dark spruce forest? Or catch the unmistakable scent of a beach at low tide? Or the tingle of cool fog droplets on our cheeks and the feel of beach gravel crunching beneath our shoes? Or the sight of an orca whale breaching as we watch through binoculars? Or simply the taste of saltwater? Young or old, something in us clicks. The explorer in us wants to explore. The artist in us wants to admire the scenery. The curiosity in us takes over and the questions come tumbling out. This book aims to answer some of those questions, while provoking many more.

Welcome to the Pacific Northwest and its magnificent Pacific Coast. Blessed with a moderate climate, our forests, rivers, estuaries, beaches, and rocky shores are available to us year-round, inviting nature encounters that vary from the mild to the wild (rest easy—this book is a guide to the mild end of that spectrum).

We are going to start with the basics. These are your first steps in experiencing and understanding what goes on in our coastal environment. This book is an introduction to some of the most common plants and animals that make the Northwest Coast unlike any other part of the world. You are going to meet and learn about a cast of characters that live here and that you will likely see on a regular basis as you spend more time exploring the scenic and natural wonders of our region. You will also learn about processes—climate, weather, tide, and currents—that make the Pacific Northwest Coast so productive. Along the way (and crucially), you will also learn about some of its conservation challenges and success stories and how you can do your part to protect our precious natural heritage.

The great writer and conservationist John Muir once said, "When one tugs at a single thing in nature, he finds it attached to the rest of the world." In this book we are going to tug on common plants and animals and find out what they are attached to. We are going to start with the things you will almost always see—and see what they tell us about everything else.

Many common animals and plants are important simply because they are abundant. They have survived and thrived because they have

Who can resist playing in the waves?

adapted to conditions such as geology, climate, or ocean currents—unique evolutionary strategies that give them survival advantages over competitors in this environment. Or they've persevered because they are remnant populations isolated in space and time. Common animals and plants play important roles in ecosystems and natural communities, perhaps as a top predator, if an animal, or a dominant forest species, if a tree. They actively play a role in shaping the composition of life and influencing other living species around them. Some, like orca whales, may be in danger because of environmental or human threats. Some, like *Spartina* (cordgrass), an introduced estuary plant, endanger other species by their aggressive spread. All, in some way or another, are important pieces in the mosaic of living things that call the Pacific Northwest Coast home.

Forces That Shape the Coast

Land, air, and water all meet on the Pacific Northwest Coast to create an environment unlike any other. Rugged coastal mountains, a moderating ocean-driven climate, and the forces of the planet's largest named ocean combine here to create biodiversity and ecological abundance. Before we sample some of the creatures and their habitats that make the Pacific Northwest so rich and unique, we should know a little about the place itself and the forces that shape it.

Basalt, formed on the spreading center of the Juan de Fuca Plate, inches landward, creating massive tectonic forces that lift the coastline and power the Cascade volcanoes.

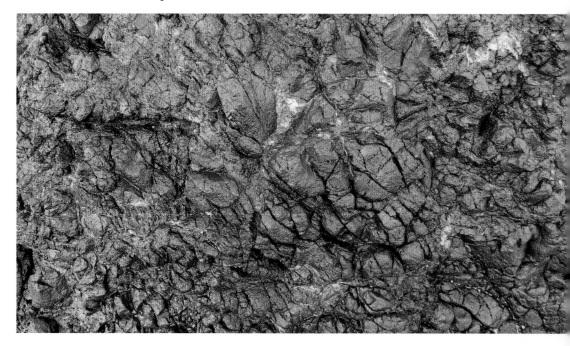

Earth's Crust and Tectonic Plates

In the Pacific Northwest, we live in one of Earth's most active tectonic areas. Not only do we get to witness an ongoing collision between an oceanic plate and the North American plate, we are at the heart of a plate breakup—a process that has gone on for millions of years as the once-vast Farallon Plate broke into separate plates. In our region, the fragments became the Explorer, the Juan de Fuca, and the Gorda Plates. Their formation, according to theory, is due to the irregular shape of the western edge of North America. Lateral stresses in crust caused it to break along lines perpendicular to the continental edge. Most of the Farallon Plate now resides deep beneath the western third of North America. Its North American remnants, the Explorer Plate, off northern Vancouver Island, the Juan de Fuca, off Washington and Oregon, and the Gorda Plate, off northern California, continue to slip beneath the edge of the continent.

Since Earth's formation, land and sea have been bound together. The ocean, where life on the planet began, shapes our climate and furnishes bounty to sustain living things, including us.

Their slow collision with North America produces periodic (in geologic time) eruptions of the Cascade volcanoes and the ever-present threat of earthquakes, great and small.

To picture Earth's crust, peel an orange very carefully. If you can, reconstruct the orange with just the peel. It's tricky without the flesh inside supporting it. Those chunks of orange peel are like Earth's tectonic plates—pieces of crust that form the outermost layer of the planet. Disconnected from each other, they want to slide around, collapse, overlap, and change shape. Driven by the slow circulation of molten rock beneath them, the tectonic plates are constantly in motion at a speed roughly equivalent to the growth of your fingernails.

Of all Earth's tectonic plates, those beneath the ocean plate are the youngest and thinnest. They are formed as liquid rock oozes out of the mantle along long, undersea mountain ranges (mid-ocean ridges) in the ocean basins. This creates a conveyor belt of volcanic rock moving away from the ridge in both directions. Typically, oceanic crust is only 4–5 miles thick. As the oceanic plates spread away from the mid-ocean ridge, they eventually collide with the continental plates, which are lighter in density and vary from 20–30 miles in thickness. Something's got to give. In most cases, the heavier ocean crust is pushed beneath the lighter, more buoyant continental crust. As the oceanic crust remelts from heat in the mantle, some of it rises through the rock above, forming active volcano chains, like the Cascade Mountains.

Pacific Northwest Coastal Geology

Although the Pacific Northwest Coast has been shaped by vast tectonic forces, regional differences account for the coastal features. The geology of the shores of Vancouver Island and the islands of the northern Salish Sea differ greatly from those of the Olympic Peninsula, the Oregon coast and northern California.

Vancouver Island and the Gulf and San Juan Islands, with their hard, exposed bedrock, are among the oldest rocks of the Pacific Northwest coastline. They have also traveled the farthest to get here. Originating as far-off island arcs, tectonic action pushed them toward

This scallop shows few signs of change from its fossilized ancestor over the millions of years that separate them.

All along the Pacific Northwest Coast, where sedimentary rocks line the shore, there is evidence of marine organisms alive between 5 and 23 million years ago.

an inevitable collision with North America. Arriving about 100 million years ago, they plastered themselves against the continental edge. Good examples of these rocks line Vancouver Island and are found throughout the San Juans and eastward to Fidalgo and Whidby Islands.

The Olympic Peninsula is younger and is the product of a more recent collision—this one between spreading seafloor basalts along with continental shelf sedimentary rocks and the North American plate. Formed about 50 million years ago, offshore sediments of sandstone, shale, and oceanic seafloor basalt were scraped off by the North American plate edge, rather than descending beneath it. Driven by the conveyor belt of spreading seafloor at the Juan de Fuca Ridge, the rocks rose to become the Olympic Mountains. Basalt lines portions of the Strait of Juan de Fuca; the outer Olympic Coast is composed mostly of softer sandstones, formed on the continental shelf.

Oregon's northern coast is lined with volcanic basalts originating not in the ocean, but far inland. The rocks that form the towering capes and headlands were all part of the massive inland eruptions that produced vast sheets of fast-flowing lava pouring from vents near what is now the Blue Mountains. Repeated flows scorched what is now the Columbia Basin, and flowed along the route of the ancestral Columbia River. These Columbia flood basalts eventually covered much of eastern Oregon and Washington and flowed into the Pacific. Towering Saddle Mountain, near Astoria, is an inland remnant. Tillamook Head, Cape Meares, Cape Lookout, Yaquina Head, and picturesque Haystack Rock, at Cannon Beach, are formed from rock produced during these unimaginably vast inland eruptions.

Softer sedimentary rocks line the central Oregon coast. These sedimentary rocks originated on the continental shelf and have been uplifted by tectonic movement that drives Oregon's Cascade volcanoes. Because of their soft properties, these coastal rocks have eroded steadily, producing the sand that lines the coastline and eventually moves ashore and inland as dunes. Cape Kiwanda, unlike major headlands to the north and south, is composed of these sediments.

Sandstones, formed on the Continental Shelf over millions of years, have been lifted and warped by movement of the Juan de Fuca Plate.

The rocks of Vancouver Island and the Gulf and San Juan Islands were formed as an island arc over 100 million years ago.

Columbia Basin flood basalts formed Saddle Mountain's rocks (following spread) and other parts of Oregon's Coast Range and prominent capes along the coast, including Cape Meares.

Windblown sand moves inland to create Oregon's famed seashore dunes.

The soft sedimentary rock of Cape Kiwanda and its dune field.

From southern Oregon into northern California, the coast is bordered by the Klamath Mountains, and composed of rocks that, like those of Vancouver Island, originated as island arcs that collided with North America sometime between 130 and 250 million years ago. In Humboldt County, the coastline softens, with marine sedimentary rocks lining the beaches and forming the forested foothills that rise into the coastal ranges of northern California.

The Maritime Climate

The Pacific Northwest—especially its coastal region—is famous for its weather. Just ask anyone who lives here to describe life in our Northwest in one word. Chances are that word will be *rain*. We sympathize with each other during the long gray winters because of the rain, and urge outsiders to reconsider moving here for the same reason, but in our hearts, we recognize the gifts of precipitation and living next to a moderating ocean that feeds us, bathes our landscape, and produces such ecological marvels on sea and land.

Our maritime climate (long-term cycle) means that conditions here are moderate by most standards. Centered roughly halfway between the Equator and the North Pole, we can expect annual average temperatures that aren't too hot or too cold. Ocean temperatures remain fairly constant

Gold Bluffs, in Prairie Creek Redwoods State Park, are soft sedimentary rocks. Early gold seekers prospected the cliffs and beaches in hopes of fortune.

The rocky headlands along the redwood coast form moody, sweeping vistas, like this view above Enderts Beach, Redwood National Park.

(45–55°F, on average) and have a steadying influence on air temperatures. As a result, seasonal temperature ranges are fairly steady—again, not too hot and not too cold, compared to interior parts of North America. Our weather (short-term cycle) is also moderate. Seasonal weather patterns of the Pacific Northwest Coast bring us low-pressure systems with lots of rain and snow in the mountains (carried from tropical regions in the Pacific) during winter. In summer, we experience high-pressure systems that bring us sunny, clear, and warm days. The combination of climate and weather cycles creates patterns that have been fairly constant for thousands of years, yet provide contrast and variation week to week, season to season, and year to year.

These patterns—and their predictability—have made this region one of the most productive coastal regions on Earth. Seafood from the ocean, timber from our forests, rain for our crops, electricity from dams, and a "just right" climate furnish us a hospitable place to live, and an abundance of living organisms—plants and animals—to feed, clothe, and shelter us.

The Pacific Northwest's climate is formed by moist ocean air rising above the coastal mountains. Precipitation, in the forms of snow, rain, and fog, give the region its reputation for dampness and an abundant supply of water to keep the region evergreen. Glaciers on Mount Carrie (center) and Mount Olympus (hiding to the right) are liquid storehouses that nourish coastal rivers. Summer fog (foreground) moderates temperatures along the coast when rain is scant.

Pacific Northwest coastal forests are among North America's wettest. The Hoh Rain Forest, in Olympic National Park, receives between 12 and 14 feet of rainfall each year.

Ocean Currents

Water never sits still. The water molecule (good old H_2O) is inherently unstable, comprised of two hydrogen atoms and one of oxygen. Lopsided in appearance, it tumbles constantly, slipping past other water molecules. It is constantly moving from the force of gravity, the rotation of Earth, and the influences exerted by the Sun and Moon, wind, currents, and the movement and shape of land (or seafloor) upon which it sits. First, let's consider ocean currents and how they affect the Pacific Northwest.

The prevailing ocean circulation pattern (or gyre) of the North Pacific is the Japan Current, so named because it moves northward along the Asian coast and is bent eastward to shoot across the Pacific toward North America, where it strikes and splits. One leg moves toward California (the California Current), one toward Alaska. That the Japan Current is a conveyor belt to our shores is attested by marine debris that carried docks, a motorcycle, and untold tons of flotsam to North America and made Japan's recent tragic earthquake and tsunami tangible on our shores as a reminder of our human family and ocean connections.

The California Current gives the Pacific Northwest Coast many of its shared physical, chemical, and biological characteristics. As a transporter of vast amounts of water, it influences the ocean ecosystem of a huge

Sun, moon, wind, and tide all combine to create the dynamic forces of the ocean.

The Juan de Fuca Eddy and the Columbia Plume

While large-scale forces, such as the major circulating currents, create a degree of stability all along the California Current, localized influences play a role in influencing the system on a more regional scale.

The Juan de Fuca Eddy (affectionately known as the Big Eddy) is the name given to the circular movement of water off the entrance to the Strait of Juan de Fuca. At the strait's entrance, water is exchanged between the combined bodies of Georgia Strait and Puget Sound and the Pacific Ocean. During a typical spring season, the combined river flow reaching the Pacific Ocean is about 5 million gallons per second. Water leaving the inland straits is rich in nutrients from vast inland landscape drained by Canada's Fraser River and all rivers that empty into Puget Sound. Where the waters meet and circulate, localized currents, coupled with coastal upwelling (vertical mixing of water near the surface), drive astonishing biological productivity, making the areas off the Olympic Peninsula and Vancouver Island ecological hot spots.

Similarly, the Columbia River adds about 2.5 million gallons per second, bringing nutrients from the far reaches of the Rocky Mountains and Columbia Basin. Both the Strait of Juan de Fuca and Columbia River produce plumes (columns of one fluid moving through another) of relatively lighter and less-salty water, laden with nutrients. In each case, the plumes spread northward and southward as they are carried by currents and counter currents.

The northern Salish Sea from Saturna Island. Localized currents are created by tidal action through passages and among islands.

The South Jetty on the Columbia River mouth receives a pounding. Jetties were formed to stabilize shifting bars across river and estuary entrances. The Columbia River's plume of sediment moves farther out to sea as a result.

region, creating similar conditions along its entire length and allowing some species to occupy ranges from the Gulf of Alaska to Baja California.

The California Current isn't constant. During winter months a weaker counter-current, the Davidson Current, flows northward along the West Coast, just shoreward of the California Current. Occasionally, El Niño conditions—which form in Equatorial regions of the Pacific—affect the Pacific Northwest. In El Niño years, warmer, tropical water spreads northward along the coast, changing seawater temperature and chemistry and disrupting the ecological patterns of distribution, food availability, and migration of many marine organisms.

Upwelling

Upwelling is the vertical mixing of water near the surface—where light penetrates. In addition to driving marine food chains, it is the force that creates the Pacific Northwest's chilly coastal fog in summer.

In the Pacific Northwest, upwelling is caused by two different mechanisms. One, common in the straits, channels, and bays of the Salish Sea (Puget Sound and the Strait of Georgia), is simply the mixing effect of currents and tides forcing water through narrows or over sills that separate different basins. The other, coastal upwelling, is driven by prevailing winds and Earth's rotation. By either mechanism, cold water mixes with warm and deep water mixes with shallow. These processes make the Pacific Northwest coastal and inland waters among the most productive in the world.

The Salish Sea has many passages among islands and deeper basins, remnants of the carving action of the Ice Age. Water that moves through these channels—pushed in and out by tides and the steady inflow from the region's rivers—keep this water moving. Places like Active Pass in the Gulf Islands off Vancouver Island and Deception Pass between Whidbey and Fidalgo Islands look like rivers when tides are running. In this turbulence, the water mixes nutrients. The result is explosive growth of plankton, the first living link in the food chain.

Out in the Pacific Ocean, coastal upwelling is the mixing process that drives ocean productivity. During summer months, winds fare usually from the north, and water close to the coast is pushed south and nudged offshore by Earth's rotation. As the warmer inshore waters move away from land, cold water rises along the Continental Shelf to take its place. With it come nutrients that have settled in the deep water. In this form of vertical mixing, the deep water rises to the sunlit shallows creating perfect conditions for phytoplankton (tiny plants that produce their own food from sunlight) and living things on up the food chain. Upwelling is strongest during summer and causes the dense marine fog we experience at the beach. Don't worry—it is still summer a short distance from the shore.

The marine layer fog common during summer months at Pillar Point, Strait of Juan de Fuca. Cold water meets warm, moist summer air. The result: cool weather that calls for a jacket.

Surging currents boil through Deception Pass in the northern Salish Sea.

Waves

Whether you are a Pacific Northwest cold water surfer or a barefoot kid playing in the foam, waves are your constant companion on the shore. They mesmerize us with their power and rhythm, lift and propel us when we surf, knock us over when we are not watching, pound and reduce rock to particle, and carry sediments along the shore. To understand the dynamics of wave and shore, we start with waves themselves.

The birth of a wind wave is a puff of air on calm water. Tiny wrinkles appear on the surface and flow over the water, created by friction on the water's skin and weakening of surface tension. The ripples are irregular, just as the force of the wind rises and falls with gusts. When the waves begin to form a slight chop, the surface undulates, creating vertical relief that catches the wind, like a sail. And, like a boat propelled by a sail, the water moves horizontally. The higher the wave, the bigger the sail, the more wind it catches, and the more water gets set in motion. The wave grows. If it grows too high, it collapses on itself, forming a whitecap.

Soon, bigger waves begin to swallow smaller ones, absorbing their energy and becoming swells. The height and distance between swell crests

A light wind brushes the water's surface, creating small wavelets. Over distance, they grow, forming into waves and swells.

take on a uniform appearance and form even pulses of wave energy that can travel long distances without the loss of much of the wave energy.

The area in which waves form is called a fetch. A fetch's size is important in determining its wave-generating capacity. Considered as a fetch, the North Pacific is vast. As storm systems roam over the ocean, they create wave systems that radiate outward. A storm forming near Hawaii can generate waves well into the North Pacific, eventually reaching the Pacific Northwest. Experienced weather watchers like surfers and snowboarders often monitor developing storm systems long before they arrive using websites from the National Oceanic and Atmospheric Administration (NOAA) and others. A strong southwestern swell can foretell good surf conditions on the coast. If the swell comes in winter, it can signal good snow in the mountains—perfect conditions for winter sports.

Things get interesting as waves approach the shore. Swells carry wave energy well below the sea surface. As the swell encounters a rising seafloor, such as a reef, water is forced higher, producing higher waves. If the swells encounter a point or headland, waves form near that obstacle and

A long journey across the Pacific brings waves to the Pacific Northwest shore.

Tsunamis

The Pacific Northwest Coast is tsunami country. Situated along one of Earth's most active seismic zones, it has been transformed by many dramatic earthquakes throughout geologic time. The cause is a massive fault that marks the boundary between the Pacific and North American tectonic plates and lies deep beneath the coastal region. Over time, areas of our coastline have risen and fallen many times from the violent shuddering of great quakes. An earthquake in 1700 displaced areas of the Washington coast by about two yards. Its accompanying tsunami devastated villages in coastal Japan. Likewise, earthquakes in Japan and Alaska have produced tsunamis of great magnitude that reached Pacific Northwest shores, reaching far into coastal inlets and, since human time, affecting villages, cities, and ports.

Being "tsunami-safe" is a good idea anywhere along our coast. Beaches, harbors, and low-lying areas around estuaries could easily be inundated in a tsunami. A large local earthquake could cause a tsunami almost immediately. An earthquake elsewhere on the Pacific Rim could generate a tsunami that could take hours to reach our shores. In the Pacific Northwest, federal, state, and local agencies have developed warning systems and escape routes in most seaside communities. If you feel the ground shake, move to higher ground immediately. But even if the earthquake is far across the ocean and there is plenty of warning, evacuate when instructed.

Low-elevation areas of the Pacific Northwest Coast have a history of major tsunamis. Look for these signs in tsunami country. Move quickly if you feel an earthquake. Tsunamis from distant earthquakes can be just as devastating, but offer more warning.

the entire wave train bends around the point or headland. Look for this bending, or wave refraction, from any high vantage point.

Once the wave reaches the shore, its energy is forced into less and less water. The wave gets higher and the water takes on a circular, rolling motion. Forced even higher by the rising seabed, the motion becomes elliptical, with the friction of the bottom slowing the wave. The oval of the water's motion becomes top-heavy and crashes forward. Surf's up!

Inevitably, the wave energy simply runs out of water and spills onto *terra firma* (dry land)—and it packs a wallop. The energy is easily dissipated on broad sand beaches, but on hard rock—sea cliffs, headlands, and sea stacks—its force dislodges loose fragments and drives compressed air into fissures, fracturing the rock further.

Tides

The rising and falling of tides gives the seashore some of its most unique qualities. Physically, this shape-shifting reveals, then hides, large landscapes. Biologically, it creates ever-changing conditions that shoreline organisms—be they clams or crows—must adapt to in order to survive. For nature explorers like us, however, it means opportunity and danger— opportunity to enter the otherwise submerged world teeming with marine life; and danger, because our inattention can get us into trouble.

Water and mud: extremes of high and low tides illustrated near the mouth of Dungeness River on Washington's Olympic Peninsula.

Tides cycle twice daily, creating two high and two low tides in a 24-hour, 50-minute lunar day. In the Pacific Northwest, one high tide is typically higher than the other. Similarly, one low tide is lower than the other. Across the geographic range of the Northwest, differences between high and low tides vary. The mean annual tidal range is the approximate difference between high and low tides for a given location. Tidal ranges are typically greater in the north. For Tofino, British Columbia, at approximately 49 degrees north latitude, that range is about 12 feet; for Crescent City, California, at about 41.75 degrees north latitude, it's about 14 feet. Astoria, roughly midway at 46.1 degrees north latitude, has a mean annual range of 6 feet.

Tidal range in the Pacific Northwest is perfect for visiting tide pools and looking for intertidal creatures. The daily movement of the water means we can visit habitats otherwise available only to snorkelers and divers—and marine organisms. It also means we have to be very attentive to the cycles of tide. Use a tide table to find the best time for tide pooling. Just remember that absolute low tide happens only for moments; visiting two hours before and two hours after gives you plenty of time for exploration as well as the chance to notice the changes that occur when the tide turns.

Ocean Conservation

We can all do our part for ocean conservation. It begins when we figure out that we are connected to our ocean, the living things in it, and through them, everybody and everything on the planet. And we develop that connection by exploring the world around us—beaches, forests, rivers, and the natural features within our communities; by noticing things and being the curious organisms that we are; by asking questions about what we see; by learning; and by experiencing the awe of this living planet that surrounds us.

When we understand what's around us, we begin to see ourselves in our environment and understand our responsibility to protect it. We can do this through simple actions like recycling and picking up after ourselves, or not trampling tide pool animals or bothering nesting seabirds, and reminding others how they can reduce their impacts on the environment.

Our actions could also be part of something larger, like working with other people around a conservation goal, such as cleaning a beach or volunteering to organize a beach cleanup, or collecting data that helps scientists understand trends in the environment.

Wildlife Wisdom

The surest sign that you are disturbing wildlife is when an animal becomes alert to your presence and responds—with distress or warning calls, by changing behavior, or actually fleeing. As much as these behaviors are

Appreciating the
environment connects
us to life forms vastly
different from us.

survival techniques, they are also disruptive to feeding behavior, care and rearing of offspring, or simply resting. Avoiding humans can cost an animal energy and may endanger its offspring if left unprotected.

Our pets may be our best friends, but they can be pretty harmful to other animals. Natural instincts in dogs and wildlife they encounter have been honed over thousands of years. Your commands may not override a dog's urge to chase and a deer's urge to run. In some cases, dogs actually endanger their owners by arousing predators like cougars, bears, and, on Vancouver Island, wolves. Your dog running to you for protection against a pursuing black bear isn't the kind of wildlife encounter you want.

Many coastal camping areas in national and state parks are also wildlife habitat. Human campgrounds are magnets for scrounging wildlife—raccoons, deer, bears, crows, and jays. Pay close attention to campground rules about leaving coolers and food containers in camp when you are not there. Wildlife-smart camping habits save animals' lives.

Many marine animals are vulnerable to noise—sounds are greatly amplified when conducted through or over water. Whales use echolocation to navigate and communicate. Noise from boat traffic interferes with their ability to hear and causes stress for them. Seabirds can flush at loud noises, or when approached too closely. During nesting season, alert predators like crows, eagles, and gulls will swoop in on unprotected nests, eating eggs or snatching babies while the disturbed parents are away. You can learn to read animals' sensitivity to your presence by noticing their behaviors and paying attention to your proximity.

Around the House

Conservation doesn't just happen outdoors. We all live in a watershed. Did you know that what is under your kitchen sink is part of your watershed? That's right; the very place where we store cleansers and household chemicals that, if improperly used, can pollute rivers, estuaries, and the ocean. Choose less-toxic alternatives when you can and dispose of toxics properly. Most communities sponsor household hazardous waste collection days. Round up your partially used containers and dispose of them properly.

The garage is another place to check. Fertilizers and pesticides applied to lawns and garden areas can make their way into stormwater runoff—and directly into storm drains and streams. Eventually, they enter rivers and estuaries where the nutrients and toxics cause harm. Minimize the yard chemicals you use, use only according to directions, and dispose of leftovers properly.

Recycle. Sorting your recyclables—glass, plastics, aluminum, paper, and steel—gives them a head start for their next use and saves the energy and effort needed to produce the raw materials we use daily. Recycling also

Tide Pool and Trail Etiquette

People can indeed love nature to death. Many popular areas in parks and other wild areas show signs of trampling and the wear and tear of heavy human visitation. You can reduce your share of that damage by following simple rules and using common sense. Most popular natural areas post regulations and warnings that alert you to your own impacts. In many places, the rules are strictly enforced by rangers or volunteers—but not always. Not everyone knows what to do (or what *not* to do) and why.

Shoreline vegetation and soils are very vulnerable to trampling and erosion. Stick to established trails and remain behind railings and other barriers. Coastal bluff areas can be unstable, and unsafe. Never cut switchbacks—that bare soil just encourages others to follow.

Tide pools and intertidal creatures are easily damaged by trampling and careless handling. The "crunch, crunch" of hundreds of human feet on barnacle and mussel beds kills individual animals and, over time, can denude large areas of life, reducing biodiversity in intertidal habitats. Watch where you step in the intertidal zone. Choose bare rock and sand whenever possible. Avoid stepping on beds of sea anemones and other soft-bodied organisms. And be very careful around slippery seaweed. A misplaced step can cause a tumble and painful barnacle scrapes.

Hands-on learning is a good way to appreciate intertidal creatures, but careless handling injures or kills animals. Never pull an attached creature from its place on the rocks. You can easily tear off the tube feet of sea stars and injure the foot tissue of mollusks, such as snails, limpets, and chitons. Lightly, give it the tug test—if the animal resists being picked up, it's telling you to leave it alone. If you do pick up

Examining the foot on a gumboot chiton. Animals that resist being lifted are telling you, "Hands off!" Be gentle when you take a closer look.

an animal, always replace it exactly as you found it and return rocks to the position where you found them. Chances are, the tide pool critters were hiding or resting where you found them; leaving them exposed to gulls or other predators can be a death sentence.

Under no circumstances should you collect live marine animals—they thrive in the wild, not in your home aquarium or backpack. In most cases they will die off quickly when removed from their natural environments. And parks and popular tide pool areas often prohibit collecting animals by regulation. Some animals, like crabs and shellfish, require licenses for gathering and have strict size and harvest limits. Know the rules.

Finally, if you see someone else harming marine life, politely ask them not to. They may not know how their actions affect the animals and animal communities of the intertidal zone. It can be more effective to use "why" statements ("Putting it back in its place keeps it hidden from predators"), as opposed to "what" statements ("It's against the rules"). You have a chance to teach someone else to care for the marine environment, and hopefully they'll pass the message along to others.

saves on landfill space and keeps junk out of our rivers, off of the beaches, and out of the ocean.

Since the first Earth Day in 1970, we've learned hundreds of ways to reduce our environmental footprint around the house. If the idea is new to you, start with small steps. If you already practice green living habits, challenge yourself to find new ways to protect the environment from your home.

In Your Community

Several things happen when friends, neighbors, and colleagues work together on environmental projects. First, a lot gets done. Second, having everybody pitch in is a great way to build community. We are social creatures, after all. We learn from each other and we like knowing that we share values about what is good, not just for us, but for others too. Many churches, service organizations, community nonprofits, and public agencies organize events around Earth Day. Pick one (or more) and join with friends and neighbors to make your community better. Clean up a beach or a stream, plant trees, or volunteer at a nature center or park. Become a member or board member of a local environmental organization. Write letters or speak out when local environmental issues are brought before your community's elected leaders.

Volunteers help resource managers by monitoring trends in the environment. On the Washington coast, volunteers sample beaches for marine debris, measuring quantities and sorting by type to determine its possible origins.

Citizen Science

The term *citizen science* is new, but the idea isn't. Thomas Jefferson, for one, spent his whole life being a citizen scientist. His insatiable curiosity drove him to keep records of weather and other natural phenomena. He conducted experiments cultivating useful plants. Today, citizen scientists work in many environmental areas. They monitor invasive plants, migrating whales, spawning salmon, changing beach conditions, and beach wash-ups such as dead seabirds and marine debris. Citizen scientists are the local eyes and ears for resource managers and researchers. Typically, they are trained to make observations and record information, which is checked by scientists for its accuracy and to spot trends in the environment. For example, seabird monitors are frequently the

early warning system for natural events in the ocean, such as storms or feeding conditions that can kill seabirds.

Being a citizen scientist requires some training (usually free) and the discipline to follow scientific procedures reliably. But volunteers who conduct scientific activities are rewarded with much deeper knowledge of their subject matter than most lay people. Opportunities to become a citizen scientist are all around you, whether you are a young person or retiree. Check with your local park, nature center, or environmental non-profit. Chances are that with your local knowledge, eye for detail, and some training, you can make a lasting contribution to the science of our natural places.

The best contribution you can make to the marine and coastal environment of the Pacific Northwest is simply to learn about it. Ocean explorer and scientist Sylvia Earle once said, "It's not what we put in the ocean or what we take out of it that causes the most harm. It's what we don't know about the ocean that hurts it the most." This means that, yes, pollution and overharvest (removing more than the sustainable amount of a resource) are bad for the ocean—but our ignorance of the ocean is its worst enemy. Humans have the remarkable ability to learn and adjust their actions accordingly. So let's learn. And let's act. Our ocean and coasts need us all to pitch in.

A student volunteer measures the diameter of a redwood in Redwood National Park as part of a study on human impacts from trampling.

Habitats of the Pacific Northwest Coast

Coastal Forests

Coastal forests are as much a part of the Pacific Northwest seashore experience as the sand beaches or tide pools. Almost every encounter we have with the wild coastline begins as we step into the forest, pass through its vaulted canopy, break out of groves of stunted trees, take in the view from a high headland, and step out onto rock or sand.

Moist marine air and moderate temperatures—gifts of the Pacific Ocean—make the great forests of the coastal Pacific Northwest possible and some of the most productive terrestrial ecosystems on Earth. The forest belt along the Pacific Northwest Coast is home to the world's largest and heaviest trees, arboreal behemoths that, collectively, exceed every other type of forest in biomass and scale. These are the blue whales of terrestrial organisms. In this chapter, we will explore how and why, and how they connect to the ocean. We will determine, besides the trees themselves, what makes these forests so unique.

Our coastal conifer forests of redwood, Sitka spruce, western hemlock, western red cedar, and Douglas fir (the five biggies among our 25 conifer species) are products of millions of years of evolution of a living community, a unique geologic setting, and a climate system powered by the Pacific Ocean.

For hundreds of millions of years, conifers held dominance throughout the world's ecosystems. With the rise of angiosperms (plants that bear their seeds within fruit) about 25 million years ago, conifers were squeezed by the competition of these "new" plant forms, capable of reproducing under broader conditions. The conifers survived in only the harshest of environments. Within the last ten million years, as the Cascades, Coast, and Olympic Ranges rose, cooler temperatures and ocean moisture created conditions that, once again, favored conifers. A shift in ocean currents and water temperature that affected the region's climate, about 7,000 years ago, produced a warmer and wetter climate and conditions that distinctly favored conifer survival.

Moderate year-round temperatures, distinct wet and dry seasons, and long periods of cloudiness give the edge to trees that maintain their foliage year-round, are capable of surviving summer dry months, and can convert low levels of sunlight throughout the year into the sugars that sustain them. All these advantages spell success on the Pacific Northwest Coast for big trees with millions of needles capable of absorbing the diffuse light of cloudy conditions.

But it is the gift of ocean upwelling—that process that creates the bounty in marine food chains—that truly makes the giant forests possible. As odd as it may seem, giant coast redwoods and Sitka spruces and minute one-celled phytoplankton in the ocean all owe their abundance and productivity to the upwelling processes along the Pacific Northwest Coast. For

The coastal region of the Pacific Northwest produces some of the most productive forests on earth.

Coastal forests thrive in the fog belt near the Pacific Ocean. Each tree's millions of needles form perfect surfaces on which moisture condenses, cooling and quenching the forest ecosystem.

phytoplankton, the link is obvious. Cold water transports seafloor nutrients upward into the sunlit shallows during summer months when upwelling is most common. For the forests, it's a two-step process. The same cold water that delivers nutrients to plankton creates summertime fog that creeps inland to the forested coastal mountain slopes. The fog brings moisture that bathes the forests throughout the season when actual rainfall is scant.

What makes the old-growth forest so productive as habitat is the complexity of structure found in these ancient stands. Disturbance on a large scale by wind or fire allows the rapid regeneration of "pioneer species," like red alder, whose seedlings quickly dominate the new habitat and outcompete slower-growing tree species. Disturbance on a small scale due to a single tree falling and creating an opening, for example, allows for young seedlings of shade-tolerant trees like western hemlock and western red cedar to fill the gap, along with a host of smaller trees and shrubs. These disturbances continually reshape the forest in a multilayered maze of structures that support hundreds of other species.

Although we are drawn to the majesty of towering and vital-looking living trees, a tree's death (at, say, 700 years) is not the end of its story; it is perhaps only it's halfway point in contributing to the forest ecosystem. Dead snags, downed logs, stumps, and decomposed mounds of former wood fiber harbor the majority of the nutrients in the Pacific Northwest coastal forest—soils themselves are relatively poor in nutrient content.

Although many forested areas next to the coast in northern California, Oregon, Washington, and Vancouver Island have been logged at some point, significant areas remain pristine. Some due to extreme conditions that have made the forest inaccessible or uneconomical to harvest or simply stunted tree growth, others because conservationists saw the value in protecting them, along with the shores they tower over. We are fortunate to have vast tracts of old-growth forest lining our wild coast. These trees and the plant and animal communities they harbor are our greeters as we approach our shores.

Mineral soils in coastal forests are poor in nutrients. It is the centuries-old accumulation of organic matter, in stumps and downed logs, that nourishes the forest's growth.

coast redwood

Sequoia sempervirons

The leviathan of Pacific Northwest coastal forests, the coast redwood is the world's tallest tree. One California giant, named Hyperion after a Greek legend, reaches a dizzying 379 feet—the standing world record. Standing, indeed.

Coast Redwoods range from the extreme southern Oregon coast deep into the central coast of California. Nowhere do natural groves grow more than 50 miles from the coast. They thrive here as a result of the ocean's moisturizing summer fog, the product of ocean upwelling, the ecological force that drives ocean, as well as forest, productivity in the coastal Pacific Northwest.

Redwoods, by their sheer height, defy the logic of water flow. To move water 300 feet from the bottom of a household well requires a stout pump. Trees, in contrast, have no motors. Life-giving moisture is carried to the highest needles through the suction of transpiration, the breathing process of all plants. Water molecules cling to each other like train cars within minute vessels in the trees' inner bark, traveling to all the living tissues of the plant. But it can get dry up top, particularly for giant trees whose tips are fully exposed to the California sun. The evolutionary workaround for redwoods is found in their needle structure—wide needles lower on the tree are arranged in broad rows, capable of extracting the maximum of sunlight in the deep forest. Those high on the tree are arranged in tight, spiky bundles that conserve the moisture within. This maritime climate-driven adaptation illustrates the seamless connectivity between ocean and land worlds and the life they each nurture. ★

The conservation of redwoods is a historic model of success in recognizing and acting to protect our environmental legacy. Throughout the twentieth century, conservationists worked tirelessly to educate the public, and to negotiate with timber companies and governments alike, to preserve the redwoods. Nearly 200,000 acres of protected groves are the result. But preservation of trees isn't enough—logged lands and streams and other critical components of forest systems need to be actively restored. Redwood conservation offers models—and success stories—that can be applied to other imperiled ecosystems.

Redwood foliage differs according to location on the tree. Topmost needles (left) remain tightly clustered to retain moisture; lower needles fan out to absorb diffused light in the cooler lower understory.

Redwoods often grow in ringed clusters, each tree beginning as a sprout emerging from a long-gone stump.

55

Douglas squirrel

Tamiasciurus douglasii

Making up in vocalization what they lack in size, Douglas squirrels, sometimes called chickarees, are noisy in defense of their territories. Male and female pairs will occupy areas of up to 2½ acres and defend them aggressively against other squirrels. The scolding bark fills the air with staccato bleats. When you hear it, you'll know that you have trespassed into the squirrel's territory.

Stop and look for the little noisemaker. He or she has gray-brown fur with a tan or yellowish belly, a conspicuous eye-ring, and is typically sitting on a limb or clinging, spread-eagled, to a tree trunk. Move in that direction

and you will hear the frantic scratching sounds of squirrel claws running up or down or around the tree; you might even see the acrobat running along a high branch or jumping from limb to limb.

Douglas squirrels are important in forest ecology. Although they feed primarily on conifer seeds, they also eat mushrooms, truffles, berries, acorns, berries, and fruit, distributing seeds and spores throughout the forest. Look for heaps of seeds and scales of the cones of spruce, Douglas fir, shore pine, and bigleaf maples. These squirrels hoard their food in piles called middens, which, if neglected, germinate and sprout. Squirrel predators include pine martens, weasels, great horned owls, bobcats, and domestic cats.

The Douglas squirrel is common throughout Pacific Northwest forests except on Vancouver Island, where the native red squirrel (*Tamiasciurus hudsonicus*) is of a different species. The Vancouver Island squirrel's range is shrinking due to a scurrilous exotic interloper. It faces competition from the larger and more aggressive gray squirrel (*Sciurus carolinensis*), native to the Atlantic Seaboard. Introduced on Vancouver Island in 1966, when several animals escaped from a game farm, the gray squirrel continues its spread up-island, often outcompeting the native squirrels for prime habitat and territory. ★

Garry oak

Quercus garryana

Garry oak

Pacific Northwest coastal forests are primarily known for their huge conifers. Yet in the drier areas of the northeastern Olympic Peninsula, southern Vancouver Island, and the Gulf and San Juan Islands, a very different forest grows: the Garry oak woodland.

Coastal Garry oaks thrive on rocky outcrops in the dry microclimates of the "rain shadows" of Vancouver Island and the Olympic Mountains. These areas—too rocky or arid to be dominated by lush foersts—are small remnants of communities that were widespread in the Pacific Northwest some 6,000 years ago, before the rise of the modern moist, temperate climate we know now. That change

Garry oak woodlands harbor diverse communities of animals and plants. In British Columbia, oak woodlands on southern Vancouver Island and the Gulf Islands are considered one of Canada's most endangered ecosystems. Scientists believe that, as climatic warming overtakes our region, oak communities will expand as other forest communities shrink. In the changing mosaic of forested habitats, oak woodlands will become ecological lifeboats for many common species of the region.

Classic white oak leaf form and rugged checkered bark distinguish the Northwest's most common oak.

Under harsh coastal conditions, at the edge of its natural range, Garry oak assumes stunted and contorted forms. Life here is tough.

Wild oak habitat includes many shrub associates. Oregon grape is common in dry oak forests.

of climate—to a warmer, wetter one—made the conifer forests as we know them possible.

While Garry oaks of the Willamette Valley and Puget Trough are often tall and rounded in form, the coastal oaks of the islands appear stunted and gnarled due to the harshness of growing conditions. In deeper, moister soils of wet meadows, Garry oaks can grow into stately trees, which are common in and around Victoria, British Columbia. In wilder environs, such as the Gulf and San Juan Islands, they are the backbone of rich habitat for birds, mammals, butterflies, and many rare plants. In Washington, over 200 species of vertebrates are known to use Garry oak woodlands as habitat. Snowberry, Nootka rose, tall Oregon grape, and sword fern are common oak associates. ★

Pacific banana slug

Ariolimax columbianus

The Pacific banana slug is one of the most common and most easily recognized animals in the Pacific Northwest coastal forest. Don't worry about being quick enough to catch a glimpse, because these shell-less land mollusks never go anywhere in a hurry. Once you get past the yuck factor, they are remarkable animals that play a critical role in forest ecology.

Our common banana slug can reach up to 9 inches in length. In addition to the brilliant yellow color, individuals can be green, olive, spotted with black splotches, or even entirely black. Food preference explains the color differences. They slowly creep along through leaves and forest debris on slime trails exuded from specialized glands in their bodies—highways of their own construction that provide a smooth surface for their soft bodies.

Banana slug sex is not like that of most animals. Individual slugs have the reproductive organs of both sexes. Courtship involves circling each other in an S shape before finally clinging together for the passage of sperm to egg. About 30 eggs are produced, deposited in a crevice or protected space within debris of the forest floor or decomposing logs. Baby slugs emerge about eight weeks later. Both eggs and tiny slugs are easy prey for shrews, birds, and other predators.

Slugs' roles in the forest ecosystem are profound. They form one of the final stages of the recycling process of forest nutrients. As they roam along on their silver thoroughfares, they use a radula, or toothed tongue, to rasp bits of debris, minute algae, and other products of decomposition. Passing it through their digestive system, the waste product is almost pure humus. Thus trees, the mighty giants of the forest, along with everything else that has lived and eventually died, are broken down into fine particles and become part of the forest soil. ★

Banana slugs range from bright yellow to dull olive. Many have spots. Scientists believe that coloration may be due to diet, age, and the health condition of the animal.

pileated woodpecker
Dryocopus pileatus

pileated woodpecker

Large squarish holes have been carved in a snag and wood splinters lie on the ground below: the signs of a pileated woodpecker's industry and skill as a winged woodcarver. Our largest woodpecker doesn't just peck, it chisels, gouges, wedges, and splinters living and dead tree trunks in search of its favorite food: carpenter ants and other wood-dwelling insects.

The pileated woodpecker is easy to identify by its showy red crest, boldly striped black and white body and head and bright eye. Its call, a machine-gun series of insistent cheeps, and the sound of its woodwork, more like chopping than pecking, ring through the woods. In flight on its broad wings, it rises and falls in an undulating path through the understory.

Pileated woodpeckers require forest habitat with a mix of healthy trees and large snags—which easily describes many of our coastal forests. Mating pairs occupy large territories of up to 175 acres and remain in the same vicinity year-round and from year to year. During breeding season, they are particularly aggressive toward other pileated woodpeckers, chasing them away and drumming on trees to declare their territory. Males do much of the nest-building woodwork, carving deep holes that reach 10–20 inches into rotting wood. Females lay a clutch of three to five eggs, which hatch after about 18 days. The nestlings remain for up to 28 days before leaving to establish their own territories. The parents then abandon the nest cavity. Once they vacate, the holes attract many other species of forest wildlife, including owls, bats, and small mammals.

Pileated woodpeckers are the woodcarvers of the forest. Many other animals use the holes once the birds move out.

Pileated woodpeckers require habitat with a mix of healthy trees and large, decaying snags, a characteristic of old-growth forests. They actively modify their habitat by creating feeding and nesting space for many other species. In a healthy forest, they are considered an indicator species—their presence is evidence of an adequate supply of dead and decaying trees, as well as abundant habitat for a host of other forest insects, birds, and mammals. Conservation-minded foresters have taken note. Many harvested forests have "leave trees," trees of lesser market value, but which can grow and die to become the next generation of snags, furnishing future generations of wildlife with adequate dead and dying trees, even as a young, thriving forest grows up around them.

Roosevelt elk

Cervus elaphus

The largest member of the deer family living in Pacific Northwest coastal forests is the regal Roosevelt elk, the name given to the coastal Northwest's subspecies, considered distinct from other North American elk. Elk once ranged over much of North America, but changes in habitat have reduced their range significantly.

Males can weigh as much as 850 pounds or more and each year produce large antlers that are shed during late winter months. Males and females are similar in color, with deep brown heads, pale brown bodies, and light tan rumps. Calves are born in May and June, weighing about 35 pounds and losing their spots within a few months. By its first winter, a calf may weigh over 200 pounds, nourished by rich mother's milk.

Roosevelt elk are considered grazers (eaters of grass). However, in forest habitats they eat a varied diet that includes shrubs, tree shoots, and many species of ground cover, including grass. Although elk have been popularized as migratory animals, Roosevelt elk that inhabit temperate coastal forests and river valleys often do not migrate any great distance where year-round food, in the form of forest forage, is available. Some movement between river valleys and adjacent ridgelines takes place, but herds tend to remain localized.

Elk spend most of their lives in small herds of cows, young males, cow-calf combinations, and bulls. Mature males often form bachelor herds during part of the year. During the autumn rut, the sound of elk bugling can fill the woods, even if dense cover makes them hard to see. Dawn and dusk are when the animals are most active. Look (and listen) in old-growth forests, logging clear-cuts, river bars, farm fields, abandoned orchards, and even coastal dunes. Be cautious during hunting season—you aren't the only one stalking this wild quarry. It's a good idea to don a blaze orange vest or jacket or limit your own elk "hunting" to national parks and other areas where the animals are protected.

Roosevelt elk

Hunted nearly to extinction in the early 1900s, Roosevelt elk gained legal protection through the work of many conservationists, including President Theodore Roosevelt. The earliest version of what was to become Olympic National Park was actually called Elk National Monument, designated within the Olympic Forest Reserve, specifically to protect them. Today, herds are abundant in coastal areas and can be seen in many national and state parks, state wildlife areas, as well as coastal farming areas adjacent to forested land.

Coastal Roosevelt elk browse on a variety of grasses, herbs, and shrubs. Lowland herds migrate only short distances as mild weather conditions provide year-round shelter and forage in coastal forests.

rough-skinned newt

Taricha granulose

The coastal forests of the Pacific Northwest are thankfully short on poisonous snakes—or other toxic creatures, for that matter—with one important exception: the rough-skinned newt. Common throughout their range, we encounter them often. They are docile, slow moving, even attractive, with curious-looking faces and a broad grin. And fortunately, they don't bite. They are only poisonous when eaten—very poisonous. It is estimated that a single newt contains enough toxin to kill 25,000 mice. Toxins in one newt could kill a human.

The rough-skinned newt is a stocky salamander with finely grained brown or reddish-brown skin. The underside is bright orange—a danger sign to would-be predators. When threatened, the newt raises its chin and tail and arches its back as a warning. The only predators known to have resistance to the newt's toxin are certain populations of garter snakes.

Adults live most of their lives on land, foraging in the forest litter. When their springtime breeding season arrives, they head for water. The males congregate in ponds, lakes, streams, and side channels. In their water habitat, the males change physically. Their tails flatten into a long swim fin and their skin loses its roughness, becoming shiny and smooth. Once the females get to water, breeding begins. Egg masses remain in the water until they hatch, producing young newts with long fins on their backs ending in pointed tails. These larval forms also display branched gills. After a period that can extend into the next year, the juveniles move away from water and reside in the forest. Newts can live for up to 12 years.

While rough-skinned newts are easy to catch and examine, it is not advisable. If you do insist on picking one up, make sure to wear gloves and have no cuts or open sores. Wash your hands thoroughly afterward. ⭐

salal

Gaultheria shallon

Salal berries ripen to a rich purple. Dried and pounded, they were a staple for Northwest Natives.

Coastal forests, particularly those on windblown clifftops where the sound of breaking waves accompanies bird songs, are dense with shrubs. Most common among them is salal, an evergreen bush with glossy green egg-shaped leaves the size of large potato chips. Look closely at the veined leaves to see the minute saw teeth lining the edges.

Dense tangles of salal, combined with downed logs and branches, make the forest an impenetrable thicket—perfect habitat for reclusive forest birds, mammals, amphibians, and insects. Salal stands often reach over head height in the shore environment, supported by tough woody stems that seem to reach across as much as up to support their leafy canopies. Salal has deep, fibrous roots that bind forest soils together. Where fire clears a forest understory, salal will rapidly resprout with vigorous new shoots of pale green leaves.

Salal tolerates a wide range of habitats, from fairly dry soils to fairly wet ones. On the dry side, salal is an important shrub in dunes, where salal stands are a transitional community in space and time. Along with evergreen huckleberries, they form a shrub community that bridges communities of early dune colonizers, such as beachgrass and many herbs, as well as the steady encroachment of shore pine and successive forests of spruce and hemlock that dominate later. In wetter environments like coastal bogs, salal forms dense clumps, readily taking root in acidic bog soils.

Salal is part of the large heath family, which includes mountain heathers, huckleberries, rhododendrons, and even the madrone (*Arbutus*) tree. Salal blossoms are small, pinkish urns that dangle from the branch tips. These develop into deep blue or purple berries that are edible, used by indigenous people as semi-dry compressed cakes, and savored by foragers today in pies, jams, and preserves. ★

Salal was introduced in England by Scottish botanist David Douglas, one of the Pacific Northwest's first scientific explorers. Considered desirable at first, it spread rapidly, threatening native heath habitats by overwhelming and smothering native species.

shore pine

Pinus contorta subsp. *contorta*

Shore pine is the common name for one of several subspecies of lodge-pole pine, a tree that grows over a vast range that extends from the West Coast to the Rockies, covering much of British Columbia and reaching south into Sierra Nevada of California. Look for shore pines in coastal dune areas, especially along sand spits and in forest-covered dunes.

The coastal subspecies differs from its interior relatives in its form; it tends to be very branchy and rounded. Like other lodgepole pines, its needles are arranged in bundles of two, but are shorter and more densely packed along the branches. The trees have thick, rough bark and produce seeds eaten by many birds and mammals.

Shore pines illustrate patterns of change over time (known as succession). On the time scale of thousands of years, lodgepole pines were probably the first conifers to colonize areas immediately following the Ice Age, when climatic conditions were colder and drier in the Pacific Northwest. Our shore pine forests probably gained their foothold at that time, shrinking as climate and plant communities changed.

On a time scale of decades, shore pines are the first conifers to colonize coastal sand dunes because of their resistance to salt spray and their ability to thrive where other trees cannot. As they grow, they stabilize soils, but, more importantly, they provide

cover for other shrub and tree species, including Sitka spruce. Eventually, the Sitka spruces outgrow the pines, shading them and blocking pine seed germination.

Mixed forests of shore pine and Sitka spruce occur all along the Pacific Northwest Coast. On Oregon's coast, shore pines and rhododendrons form a beautiful forest community. Shore pines are also common in coastal bogs. Here, they grow in stunted forms, scattered through the bog among spruce, Western red cedar, huckleberry, Labrador tea, sundew, and other plants that thrive in the moist, acidic soils of these peat habitats. ★

Shore pine outcompetes other conifers in harsh coastal environments like sand dunes ⬇ and bogs ⬆.

Sitka spruce

Picea sitchensis

Meet Sitka spruce. I mean literally— reach out and shake its hand. Instantly, you have the key to identifying this coastal tree by its prickly branch and needles. Sitka spruces are the largest spruce trees in the world, reaching up to 300 feet in height. Their natural range coincides precisely with the coastal fog belt of the Pacific Northwest, all the way to Alaska. Although they are present in the temperate rainforest valleys of the Klamath, Coast Range, and Olympic Mountains, as well as low-elevation valleys of the Western Cascades around Puget Sound, they dominate the forests of the ocean shore itself. Here, they hug the clifftops in ragged and wind-sculpted forms and stand as dark sentinels from the spray zone of the beach high onto the coastal bluffs and headland slopes.

In addition to its prickly handshake, Sitka spruce can be identified by its plated silver-gray bark and blue-green foliage. The cones are densely packed with thin, spiraling scales. Spruce wood is light in weight and very strong, which made it ideal for airplane construction in the World War I biplane era. More recently, its resonant qualities make it highly desirable for guitars and violins.

On thin forest soils, Sitka spruce produce broad, shallow root structures. Trees that have toppled in heavy windstorms (common in winter) reveal complex, and sometimes massive, lattices of interwoven roots that once nourished and supported the tree.

Like the coast redwood to the south, Sitka spruce's dominion in the coastal region is due to its ability to harvest fog—the most common form of summer precipitation. Each tree's millions of individual pin-like needles collectively form a vast surface area upon which moisture particles can condense and combine into water drops. This cools and dampens the foliage and, as it drips toward the ground, hydrates the whole forest community. ✴

Sitka spruce's prickly needles are the easiest way to identify the tree.

The gray, scaly bark of the Sitka spruce distinguishes it from other large coastal forest trees.

stinging nettle
Urtica dioica

If you're not paying attention, you may brush up against a stinging nettle arching into the trail. Within minutes, the back of your hand will be burning and small white welts will appear. They will burn, then itch, but thankfully soon go away. Nettles, after all, are more a nuisance than a real threat. Once stung, even small children learn to recognize and avoid them.

Moist forests and field edges are perfect nettle habitat, particularly if the soil is rich in nitrogen or has been disturbed. The plants, which form thick stands, often reach over 7 feet tall, sprouting from long, sinewy runners that lie just under the duff or leafy debris on the ground. The long fibrous stem bears its leaves in opposite pairs. Each leaf has a sawtooth edge and fine hairs. Leaves have both stinging and nonstinging hairs. Like little syringes, the stinging hairs inject chemical compounds that cause the pain we feel. Relief usually comes naturally after a few hours, but anti-itch creams can quell the symptoms. Many folk remedies have been recommended, including treating with urine, saliva, mud, baking soda, lemon juice, and various plant leaves. Wearing long sleeves, pants, and gloves—and being watchful where you step—are the best prevention measures.

Nettle produces a remarkably strong fiber, similar in quality and strength to linen. Many cultures have found ways to use nettle fiber for coarse cloth and cordage. Nettle has also been used as a traditional medicine for a host of conditions. It appears to be effective in reducing inflammation in some forms of arthritis and is available in a variety of formulations as an herbal medicine.

Nettle is also a very popular edible leafy green, when the young shoots are harvested just after emergence. Boiling eliminates the toxins and tenderizes the leaves, giving them taste and texture like spinach. It's best to pick even the young leaves with dishwashing gloves to avoid the sting. ★

sundew
Drosera rotundifolia

Coastal forests are not all dark and deep. Bogs occur where groundwater is close to the surface and sphagnum moss has accumulated over centuries to form deep peat deposits. Because the soils are so rich in organic material, they are highly acidic, and soil nitrogen levels are very low. Because of this, bog forests are stunted, with scattered shrubs and a spongy surface of sphagnum moss. Here, we look for the tiny, glistening red carnivorous plant called sundew. Look closely, they are easy to miss.

Most carnivorous plants produce sugars through photosynthesis, getting nutrition directly from sunlight. Somewhere along the line, they developed other adaptations that also let them capture, digest, and benefit from the highly concentrated proteins of insects and other animals. Specifically, sundew digests its victims' proteins with enzymes that convert them into ammonia, a chemical source of nitrogen that is lacking in bog soils.

Sundew plants grow in low rosettes up to 3 inches across, with the rounded

dew-bearing leaves growing on stems that radiate from the plant. In bloom, sundews send up a single hairless stem that bears a row of delicate and innocent-looking blossoms, themselves harmless to insects.

Sundew is too small to catch and consume anything larger than tiny insects. But the little bugs are attracted to their intense red color and their sweet and sticky nectar, which forms on tiny hairs of their round leaves. A cruel death awaits. The glue-like droplets immediately ensnare the insect's feet. As it writhes, enzymes begin to attack the legs and abdomen. The plant is literally eating it alive. Some bugs suffocate when the gummy liquid clogs the breathing pores in their body. The effort to escape only makes things worse.

Our native sundew is found in temperate bogs throughout the Northern Hemisphere and was the subject of much of Charles Darwin's speculation and experimentation on carnivorous plants. He described them once as "disguised animals." ★

Another carnivore, the pitcher plant (*Darlingtonia*), like sundew, loves bugs. Unfortunate insects tumble into the plant's yawning "pitcher" and cannot escape. Digestive enzymes break down the proteins and the bug is, well, dinner. Visit this bog just north of Florence, Oregon.

sword fern
Polystichum munitum

Our most recognizable fern is the stately sword fern, named, I imagine, for its favored use among small children—being brandished as a long blade in mock swordfights. Even though it is very common in our forests, compared to other plants it has some very uncommon characteristics: its evolutionary history, leaf structure, and its life cycle.

Sword fern is abundant throughout the coastal forest, and widespread in forests ranging throughout Western North America. It is often seen in the company of salal, but prefers the wetter parts of salal habitat and is often a plant indicator of moisture gradients occurring in forest communities.

Ferns are ancient plants. Fossils dating back to 360 million years have been found. The fossil record shows that a rapid expansion of fern types developed quickly about 145 million years ago, just as flowering plants were gaining dominance.

Descriptive terms for fern anatomy differ a bit from other plants we know. The long leaflike thing is a frond. Small leaflets that alternate along the stem of the frond are pinnae, plural for *pinna* (meaning feather). Because a frond is composed simply of opposite rows

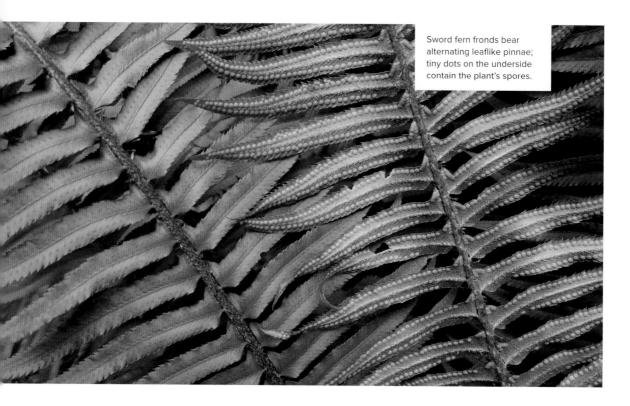

Sword fern fronds bear alternating leaflike pinnae; tiny dots on the underside contain the plant's spores.

of pinnae, sword fern is described as a single-pinnate fern. Other species display compound branching of the pinnae, making them bipinnate, or tripinnate.

Sword ferns grow as a bunch erupting out of a tough brown knot of roots. New foliage emerges as fiddleheads in spring, unfurling into handsome 4-foot fronds. Fronds typically last one or two years before dying. Sword ferns do not produce seeds. Instead, they have a complex reproductive cycle in common with other fern relatives. Look on the underside of a fern frond; on each pinna there are two rows of brown dots. These are spore cases; inside are the spores. As the plants mature, the cases open, releasing the spores into the environment where they are dispersed in the wind. Spores develop into gametophytes that produce male and female parts that, in turn, produce sperm and eggs. Once fertilization takes place on the gametophyte, a tiny fern begins growing. ★

varied thrush

Ixoreus naevius

Mornings and evenings in the coastal forest are perfect times to listen for the strange, somber song of the varied thrush. There are no complicated avian arpeggios in this melody, no wren-like vocal gymnastics inciting challenge in rivals—just a simple, vaguely dissonant combination of two notes, slurred and left to hang in the forest stillness. Repeated, the pitch will change slightly and be answered by another thrush somewhere in the distance. With this call and response, males announce their territories. Standing in one place in the forest, you may be able to hear three or four separate males at various distances, each staking his claim.

Varied thrushes are robin-sized forest birds that sport orange, brown, and gray markings. Males have a distinctive black chest band; in females the band is gray or brown. Orange lines above the eye, along the head, occur on both sexes.

Thrushes can be found year-round in our coastal areas. Some migrate short distances to higher elevations during nesting season. In winter, the locals are joined by migrants from outside the area, birds whose winter ranges are less hospitable than our mild lowland forests.

Thrushes forage on a wide range of foods. During the late summer, fall, and early winter berry season, they feast on native fruits, such as huckleberry and salmonberry. In spring and summer they consume insects and worms. Feeding on the ground, they work diligently, picking, turning, and tossing downed leaves in the forest floor litter searching for prey. Gregarious among themselves, they scatter quickly when approached, retreating into the depths of the woods.

Varied thrush nests are set low in trees, often on a branch wedged next to the tree trunk. The female will incubate three to four eggs. The hatchlings are fed by both parents. In our moderate climate, breeding pairs sometimes produce two egg clutches (set of eggs produced at one time) in a single year. ⭐

western hemlock

Tsuga heterophylla

Tolerant of a wide range of conditions, western hemlock is perhaps the most common conifer in the humid coastal forest. Hemlocks gradually gain dominance because their seedlings can grow to maturity in the shady conditions beneath the forest canopy. Where mature hemlocks occur, you should be able to find hemlocks of all ages—tiny seedlings emerging out of moss, all the way to towering monarchs of the forest. Spread by wind, the minute seeds lodge in the damp organic material of decomposing logs and stumps, producing roots that eventually thicken and form buttressed trunks as the original nurse log or stump rots away. Colonnades (neat rows) of hemlocks can be found where the seedlings once colonized a downed log that long ago melted into the forest floor as nutrient-rich humus.

The range of western hemlock includes the coastal ranges and west slopes of the Cascades and Northern Rockies between sea level and 5,000 feet. This extends well north into southeast Alaska. In California, western hemlock only thrives in a few patches on the coast, well north of the Bay Area. Western hemlock needles are rich green on top, lighter green underneath, and have distinctive white bands, which mark the lines of its stomata (tiny pores used to exchange gases). The short needles form flattened ranks along branches. Hemlock trees are easy to spot—their tops nod if you can catch a glimpse of them. The bark is thin and gray-brown with shallow furrows. Cones are small. Long a second-class citizen compared to Douglas fir as a source of timber, hemlock is now very common as a building material and source of pulp for paper.

Western hemlock shoots are important browse for deer and elk. The tender, bright green new growth is also eaten by hares. ★

Western hemlock's thin, fissured bark.

Western hemlock seedlings tolerate shade, growing in the filtered light beneath the forest canopy.

western hemlock

The small cones and needles
of western hemlock.

western redcedar
Thuja plicata

Prized for its rot-resistance and long, straight grain, western redcedar is one of the monarchs of the coastal forest. Its cinnamon-shaded bark, hanging in ragged strips, is sometimes coated with pale lichen, giving it a dusty green cast. Graceful boughs droop from the rugged trunk; sprays of needles hang off the silver limbs. Notice the individual needles—up close, they look like fine braids of waxy green cord.

Cedar likes its feet damp—we find it growing where there's water—moving in a ravine as a tumbling stream, or below the surface as seepage. On the coast, redcedar is less tolerant of salt spray than Sitka spruce, so it often shies away from the beach or rocky edge. Cedar trees, along with western hemlock and Sitka spruce, thrive as seedlings in the shaded forest. Over time, trees can reach nearly 200 feet tall and over 8 feet in diameter near the ground.

Culturally, redcedar symbolizes the natural wealth of the coastal forest. Redcedar made the Northwest Coast not just habitable, but hospitable to First Nations people. Cedar wood was split into planks to make

large houses and hollowed and carved to make canoes of all sizes. The abundance of large cedar trees gave rise to sturdy houses grouped in large permanent villages and, with seagoing canoes, the means to travel great distances between them by water and hunt the ocean for seals and whales. Easy to work, cedar is shaped into countless practical items, from combs to bent boxes—objects prominent in the material cultures of ancient and modern Northwest native people. Its fibrous bark yields material for garments and baskets; its tough roots, cordage. Today, cedar shakes, shingles, and siding clad many Northwest homes and buildings, weathering with age to a silvery patina—a signature of a common architecture of the Pacific Northwest. ★

Old-growth western redcedar, the kind that grew slowly to produce rich red heartwood and tight grains, has become scarce in managed forests because of its desirability and the intense harvest of old trees over the last century. Younger second- and third-growth wood—grown quickly and harvested young—doesn't possess the same rot resistance or working quality of old-growth wood. Today, old-growth cedar is rare in the lumber marketplace—and very expensive, if you can find it. Most surviving old-growth trees live within protected forests.

Western redcedar's scalelike needles and immature seed cones.

Cutting giant cedars with
axes and handsaws was
a monumental task for
early loggers. Holes in this
stump once supported
springboards, platforms
the loggers stood on to
make their sawcut.

Rocky Shores and Tide Pools

The coming and going of the tides makes the intertidal zones of the Pacific Northwest scenes of constant change. For animals that require water around them at all times, a rising tide provides access to new foraging territory. Fish can wander among boulders and pools otherwise unavailable to them. Limpets, crabs, and snails can roam in search of food. For animals that can tolerate exposure to air, sunlight, and warmer temperatures, a low tide is a period of inactivity where they can "close down," out of reach of underwater predators. However, low tide exposes them to other hazards: bird and mammal predators and physical stresses, like harmful ultraviolet light, drying in the sun, or freezing in cold weather.

The shores of the Pacific Northwest are relatively young. Seafloor spreading and tectonic uplift have created mountains along much of our coastline. Where this rocky terrain meets the sea, shores resist erosion but take brutal punishment from the sea. Headlands, capes, cliffs, broad terraces, headlands, offshore islands, and sea stacks are

formed as waves pound relentlessly and carve into the land. These are the forces that shape the shoreline and create the rocky intertidal zone. They shape life here as well.

Earth's elementary substances of rock and water meet on the rocky shore. The result? An explosion of life.

With the coming and going of the tide, water remains in the cracks, crevasses, and depressions, creating a mosaic of habitats—pools, kelp-covered rock terraces, and broad fields of cobble and boulders. Every surface is colonized by living organisms, whether they are plants or animals. A fixed space on the rocks provides access to food suspended in the turbulent water. A toehold in this crowded habitat is key to survival.

Constant pounding from waves means that organisms must stay attached to the rocks in order to live. Suction cup–like feet on mollusks, rootlike holdfasts on seaweeds, biological cements in barnacles, and hairy threads on mussels are all adaptations that secure them to the rocks. Tough shells protect them from impact. Animals that are mobile must weather the pounding by crawling into crevices and under rocks or the mazelike spaces among living communities like mussel and seaweed beds. During fierce winter storms, logs can batter at the intertidal zone, leaving bare patches where living communities have been pounded away by the impacts of these floating missiles. The rocks don't stay bare for long—nature's other survival trick is that many of these organisms can recolonize these areas quickly. The spores of seaweed and the larvae of barnacles, mussels, and other invertebrates resettle immediately to claim the battered territory. Snails and limpets scour the new surfaces for minute bits of fast-growing scum-like algae.

Here in the Northwest, tidal ranges are great enough to create distinct zones—horizontal bands—in the area between the highest and lowest water levels. The upper zones remain exposed most of the time; the

Rocky shorelines show
conspicuous bands—organisms
living higher on the rocks
must weather the stresses
of exposure; those living
lower risk being eaten.

lowest zones are submerged most of the time. Only extreme tides conceal or reveal these extreme areas. Each zone supports organisms adapted to the conditions of that particular zone. Typically, the lower the zone, the greater the biodiversity. But everywhere you look, you'll find amazing plants and animals.

The splash (or "spray") zone lies above all but the highest tides—but well within the range of salt spray. Because it is exposed to air most of the time, organisms that live here must be able to survive prolonged periods out of water and exposure to sun, freezing, and predators like gulls and crows and the occasional raccoon or bear. This community is usually less diverse in the number of species it supports. However, it's the zone we can visit most frequently and it can be a good starting point for exploring and getting to know the intertidal.

Common plants in the splash zone include lichens and tiny algae. Invertebrates common in the splash zone include small barnacles, limpets, snails, amphipods (small crustaceans with narrow, segmented bodies and two forms of specialized legs), isopods (small crustaceans with flat, segmented bodies), and some crabs. Birds like oystercatchers, gulls, crows, and the occasional perching bald eagle forage here.

The upper intertidal zone is exposed during most low tides. Physical stresses limit the kinds of organisms found here. We see more "marine" organisms here, but they have to be tough. The animals that remain fixed in one place must withstand extreme changes in temperature, salt content, exposure to sunlight, and drying. Animals with an advantage include animals that can retract into protective shells and shore crabs that can breathe air for short periods and have the ability to relocate to pools.

The most common seaweed is rockweed or *Fucus*. Be careful walking on these seaweed beds, as they are slippery. Take the time to look under the seaweed. Crabs and even small fish can be hiding beneath the cover of the damp seaweed, sheltered there until the next high tide.

Invertebrates common in the upper intertidal zone include many varieties of algae-grazing snails, limpets, and chitons, as well as carnivorous snails and worms. Barnacles are extremely abundant—able to open up and feed at high tide and close into their protective cone-shaped shells at low tide.

As you move into the middle intertidal zone, the diversity of seaweeds and animals increases. Look for pinkish encrusting coralline algae coating the rocks. Grazers like limpets, snails, and chitons roam freely. Sea

The upper intertidal zone teems with grazers, like chitons and barnacles, who feed at high tide by extending their feather-like legs out of their shells, capturing food particles that drift in the currents.

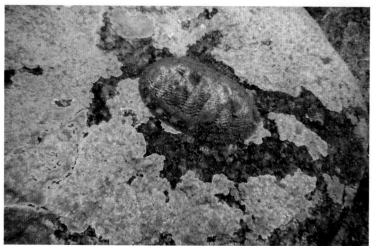

As you move lower into the intertidal, look for more life forms. This lined chiton grazes on encrusting algae.

anemones are more abundant—both the common green anemone and colonies of aggregating anemones. Mussel beds cover upper surfaces of the rocks, often interspersed with stalked goose barnacles. The lower boundary of mussel beds marks the upper limits of predatory ochre sea stars. Look for the orange and purple starfish in crevices and beneath rock overhangs.

The lower intertidal zone has the greatest diversity and is the area accessible or visible to us only during the lowest tides. Where physical stresses limit species abundance and distribution in the uppermost zones, predators determine the living order in the lowest zones. Carnivores, like sea stars, certain snails, crabs, octopus, and fish, are more abundant here. Look for sea urchins and sea anemones, clustered in sheltering cracks and fissures. Crusts of coralline algae are common on rocks and shells of some snails or limpets.

Tide pools are formed in basins and cracks in rock formations. Although most tide pools occur at the lower levels of the intertidal zone where water circulates during low tide, look for higher pools where water has been left behind by the receding tide. Pools that are perched higher in the intertidal zone may contain trapped fish and octopus, or attached organisms typically found in the lower zones.

Where pools are permanently filled with water, we get our best glimpse of the subtidal zone. This is the ocean at its shallowest. Surfgrass, seaweeds, fish, and the open "blossoms" of sea anemones reveal what life is like underwater in the ocean. Unless we don snorkel and mask and join the swimmers, this is as close as we will get. Look carefully for bright nudibranchs (sea slugs), skittering bullhead-like sculpins, reclusive octopus, or brilliant sea cucumbers, soft, fleshy relatives of sea urchins. Welcome to the ocean. Now let's get back to shore before the incoming tide catches us.

Covered by water more of the time, middle intertidal communities are diverse. Here, mussels, barnacles, and goose barnacles coexist.

Even at low tide, water remains
in pools and channels among the
rocks. These offer us a glimpse of
fish and other marine life that cannot
tolerate prolonged exposure.

black oystercatcher

Haematopus bachmani

The presence of black oystercatchers is an indicator of a healthy rocky intertidal community. First, it signals that human intrusion is relatively low and that the birds can find enough relief from people pressure. Second, it's a sign that the habitat itself is rich enough in invertebrate diversity and abundance to sustain the oystercatchers' ongoing occupation of a given territory. It's wise to pay attention to oystercatchers' distress calls, especially in nesting season. An adult forced off a clutch of eggs or away from their young leaves their next generation vulnerable to gulls, crows, and other morsel-loving predators.

Oystercatchers loudly proclaim their prescence with persistent calls as they move rock to rock in the intertidal zone. Their presence is a sign of a robust rocky shore community.

No trip to the rocky intertidal zone would be complete without complaints from black oystercatchers: "You have intruded into *my* territory." These unmistakable black birds with brilliant orange bills and pink feet nest on rocks near water's edge and are quick to scold anyone or anything that gets too close to their territory or nests. When disturbed, they fly from rock outcrop to rock outcrop, piping their shrill whistle-like call, but never venturing too far from their preferred territories.

Equipped with a tough, screwdriver-like bill, oystercatchers feed on worms and mollusks, including mussels, clams, cockles, and limpets (*not* oysters, and *definitely* not by "catching" them). They use the bill to break or pry open shells to expose the edible parts. They can also reach among and under rocks to pluck out small crabs or other invertebrates.

Oystercatchers can live up to 30 years and breeding pairs remain together for many years. Incubating the eggs and defending their home turf and nest is a shared responsibility with males and females joining together for these domestic duties. During nesting season you can sometimes spot the brooding parent atop the two- to four-egg clutch. Nearby, the mate will be sounding the alarm while the attending parent remains still.

In spite of the camouflage on both the eggs and the downy chicks, only one or two young from a given clutch survive. Within a day of hatching, the young are roaming about, being tended and fed by the parents until they fledge. After learning to fly, young birds are a duller color of black, with paler bills and feet than adults until they reach breeding age at about four years. Younger birds are usually forced away from the parents' territory. ★

A black oystercatcher feeds by using its stout bill as a pry bar to open the shells of its favorite bivalves— in this case, mussels.

California mussel

Mytilus californianus

Along the exposed outer shores of the Pacific Northwest, the most common mussel of the rocky intertidal zone is the California mussel. It is so common that it often dominates the middle to upper intertidal zone by growing in dense blue-black stands that seem to cover everything. The California mussel often reaches 8 inches in length. Its shell is composed of a pair of matched "valves," connected by a tough hinge at the pointed end. The shell has conspicuous ridges running along its length as well as concentric ridges that mark its annual growth. California mussels attach to rock and other mussels with a beard-like mass, called byssal threads. The threads are formed as a protein secretion that hardens into a tough string. Byssal threads have been studied by scientists investigating ways that human bones and tendons heal after injury. Properties of stretchiness and strength of the mussel filaments have even been considered for suturing in wounds. Mussel shells are very hard. Native American and First Nations whalers used the shell material to form blades, including razor sharp harpoon points used to hunt whales.

Mussel beds contain a lot more than mussels. In the nutrient-rich water of the intertidal zone, mussel beds become complex habitats in themselves. A 10-square-inch patch has been known to harbor over 5,000 animals of 22 species. Over time, mussels grow on mussels, trapping sediments and food particles and creating three-dimensional mazes that shelter many other invertebrates. The mussel mass thickens as young mussels grow on older ones. Look for gaps in mussel communities. Bare patches sometimes occur when the mussel stand becomes so thick that the byssal threads holding them to the rock cannot support their weight. The force of wave action, or the battering of a log or rock, can knock them off.

Mussels are filter feeders, capable of siphoning 2–3 liters of seawater per

Dense beds of mussels create structure for many other organisms. Small organisms eat minute food particles trapped among the mussel community. Barnacles attach to mussel shells themselves. And neighbors, like the goose barnacle, intertwine in the mussel thicket.

hour. Although mussels lack long tubes that protrude out of their shells, the vents that draw and expel water are just inside the broad end of the shells, near the "lips." California mussels have been a major food source for humans for millennia; however, because of the volume of water they filter, they can accumulate lethal quantities of a toxins produced by plankton. Always check local health bulletins before eating mussels, particularly during summer months.

Mussels are eaten by a wide variety of organisms, including birds, terrestrial mammals, sea stars, and snails. The predator-prey relationship with ochre sea stars (a common starfish) is so intertwined that the concept of keystone species, a central tenet of ecology, was developed based on their example. Sea star predation determines the lower boundary of mussel beds, and thus strongly influences the overall community composition of the intertidal zone. ★

Expansive beds of mussels line much of the rocky shoreline. Gaps appear when logs batter or waves shear away their threadlike attachments. The lower limit of mussel beds is determined by predators, like the ochre sea stars.

coralline algae

Family Corallinaceae

We think of marine algae mostly as brown or green plants—the long whips of bull kelp, thin sheets of sea lettuce, and even the one-celled photosynthetic plankton that makes our coastal waters so productive. But look in almost any tide pool and you will see what appears to be pink-magenta paint, dropped in blobs on many of the rocks and even the shells of snails, limpets, chitons, and other animals. Meet coralline algae—it's a plant.

Even though they lack the green pigment that we associate with chlorophyll, they are able to synthesize sunlight into sugars. But they require much less sunlight than other algae forms and can survive in very low light in cracks, crevices, and even sea caves.

The pastel crusts are really sheets of several layers of cells, growing at their edges and on their uppermost layer. With an entire layer of cells attached to the rocks, they can't be dislodged easily. In addition, they are partially composed of calcium, which makes them very tough. This combination makes them able, like few other intertidal organisms, to survive every kind of pounding.

Coralline algae are eaten by many species of grazers—limpets, snails, and chitons. That said, because of their hardness, they are very resilient to grazing. Grazers have a difficult time scraping every morsel from the surface and they grow back, slowly but surely. Many of those grazers' shells become covered by the pinkish algae crust, effectively camouflaging them against the pastel background.

If you look nearby, you will also find another form of coralline algae. Unlike the crusty type, this one grows in branching stalks like an antler or tree branch made up of small whitish-pink segments that also contain calcium. It's the same basic organism taking another form. ★

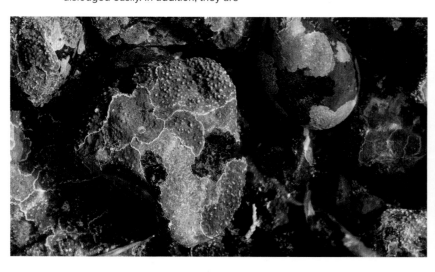

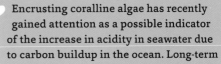

Encrusting coralline algae has recently gained attention as a possible indicator of the increase in acidity in seawater due to carbon buildup in the ocean. Long-term studies reveal that the ability of the algae to grow its calcium skeleton has been reduced by changes in ocean chemistry. Species that once were dominant because they produced skeletal cells faster than other species appear to be losing their competitive edge, a sign that coralline algae are very sensitive to ocean chemistry. Those pink splotches we see in tide pools may be a bellwether of ocean changes.

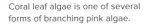

Coral leaf algae is one of several forms of branching pink algae.

giant Pacific octopus
Enteroctopus dofleini

The Pacific giant octopus is legend-ary. It is the largest octopus in the world, growing to nearly 10 feet in some cases. It is usually the star of the show in aquarium exhibits and is equally sought after and admired by Pacific Northwest scuba divers. Although octopuses usually live in the rocky recesses of deeper reefs, they occasionally make it into deeper tide pools, either stranded by a falling tide while out hunting, or crawling or wash-ing up as they die after mating.

Octopuses are cephalopods, Greek for "head-footed." Octopus relatives include squids and, in tropical waters, nautiluses. Although they are mollusks, distantly related to clams and their kin, over the course of their evolution they have lost their shells and the only hard parts of their bodies remaining are the rasp-like radula "tongue," and a birdlike beak. The radula is used to drill a small hole in the shell of prey, into which toxins are injected, killing by paralysis, and softening the ani-mal's tissue. With the beak, they cut the tissue into small bits that can pass through their esophagus. Octopuses have highly developed eyes, remark-ably similar to human eyes, consider-ing how distant we are apart on the evolutionary tree—roughly one billion years.

Octopuses are hunters, emerging from their dens to prowl among the

Octopuses die after laying their eggs. Occasionally, spawned out animals can be found in tide pools.

The octopus's arms, equipped with strong suction cups, gives it dexterity for crawling among reefs and hunting for prey.

reefs and rocks in search of prey. They are also fast swimmers, propelling themselves with water jets pumped through their siphons, and can crawl very fast, pulling themselves along with their eight arms, which are dexterous tentacles. They are typically very shy and will squeeze themselves into nooks and crannies to avoid predators. Often, the only clue that a tide pool watcher will have is a glimpse of telltale suckers on an otherwise inconspicuous reddish blob barely visible in some rock crevice.

Scientists have determined that octopuses are very intelligent. In captivity, they have learned how to travel through mazes, open jars for food, and perform certain tricks for audiences. Octopuses' skin contains many pigmentation cells, capable of a dazzling array of color changes, from light to dark reds, to white and black and even iridescent sheens. This is useful for camouflage and for baffling a predator by instantly changing appearance.

Encountered in the wild, octopuses should not be handled. Touching them damages the mucous coating on their soft tissues, making them vulnerable to infection. In addition, octopuses are capable of biting and can inject their toxic venom—the bite of a blue-ringed octopus in the tropics can kill a human within 30 minutes, if not treated. While Pacific giant octopus are not as venomous, they should nevertheless not be handled. ★

goose barnacle

Pollicipes polymerus

We are all familiar with barnacles, those little volcano-shaped shells that cover the rocks. The goose barnacle, however, grows out of a long tube stalk that projects above the rock surface, exposing the animal to nutrient-rich water that surges against the rocks. Goose barnacles are often found in clumps mingled among California mussels. They form tight clusters at their base. At the upper end of the tube, the animal is protected within an armor of five large shell plates and numerous smaller ones. Under water, the plates open and the small animal inside fans the water with its hairy legs, specialized to catch food bits.

The presence of goose barnacles within a mussel bed reveals an ever-changing dynamic in the intertidal zone. In a process scientists call succession, environmental disturbance (think crashing waves or battering logs) opens space on the rocks. At first the space is colonized by algae. Gradually, small invertebrates like barnacles take over the surface. Over time mussels recolonize the space. While there are still gaps, goose barnacles may invade and attach. They can survive among mussels because they can grow longer than the thickness of the mussel patch and dominate access to food in the swirling water. Eventually, however, pressure is too great from the mussels and the goose barnacles get crowded out.

Like mussels, their intertidal neighbor, goose barnacles are eaten by ochre sea stars. Other common predators include gulls and black oystercatchers, which pry them open with their tough specialized beaks.

In Spain and Portugal, a goose barnacle relative is considered a delicacy. Overharvest, however, has led to its scarcity. Pacific Northwest barnacles are now exported to meet epicures' demand for the delicately sweet flesh of the animal. Goose barnacles are also favored by Pacific Northwest Native People, who lovingly refer to the delicate morsels as "boots."

The pelagic (sea-going) goose barnacle lives entirely at sea, clinging to bits of wood and other floating debris. Look for them on sand beaches, where they have drifted ashore. ★

Goose barnacles can outreach surrounding mussels to get food. The mussel colony's growth eventually squeezes the barnacles out.

A related stalked barnacle lives in the open ocean, where its larvae settle and grow on drifting objects. Flotsam reaching our shore is often crowded with pelagic goose barnacles.

green sea anemone

Anthopleura xanthogrammica

Name an animal that looks like a plant that receives nutrients that come from plants (algae) that live within its tissues. Give up? Ok, it's the green sea anemone. And to make things more interesting, it's a carnivore, living primarily off small invertebrates and fish that it grasps in its rubbery tentacles and eats whole.

Sea anemones are a large group of organisms related to jellyfish and corals that grow as polyps (fleshy bud-like appendages) and possess stinging cells that they can use to immobilize prey defend themselves against predators. Most sea anemones are attached to hard surfaces, grow along a stalk—some stubby, some long—and have a "feeding disc" surrounded by tentacles, with a single opening serving as a mouth. Unlike most animals (including us), they don't have a tube running through them to form a digestive system with an entrance and an exit—theirs has just one opening where food comes in and waste goes out. Once the animal has digested all the nutrients available in its prey, it expels the leftovers—sometimes by turning its stomach cavity inside out.

Green sea anemones are especially showy when they are submerged in water. Their tentacles, like fingers, can tell the difference between food and nonfood debris even though the animal lacks what we would call a sensory system attached to a brain. They can grow to about 10 inches. Some have been recorded as reaching 100 years old.

The aggregating anemone reproduces by cloning—dividing to form another animal. Colonies of identical clones defend territories against intruding anemones from a different clone.

Sea anemones have very soft bodies and are vulnerable to trampling. At low tide, when they are exposed to air, they close up and retract into squat little clusters. If covered by sand, they are easily mistaken for rock—a place you might step on for footing. Look closely before you tread.

The aggregate anemone (*Anthopleura elegantissima*) is also very commonly seen in the intertidal zone. It is smaller and often fringed with pink. Exposed to the air, a colony looks like a rock covered with sand-covered fleshy lumps. Unlike the green sea anemone, it forms large, dense colonies by cloning itself. Each member of the colony is identical, genetically. Although they do reproduce by a spawning process, the most common strategy is by dividing into twins by pulling itself apart. When separate clone colonies encounter one another they engage in warfare using special stinging cells. As each side withdraws due to the other's attacks, a gap appears on the rock, separating the colonies by a no man's land. ⭐

gumboot chiton
Cryptochiton stelleri

Chitons are a group of mollusks that are flat and oval in shape and have eight hard plates along their back. Fossil evidence suggests that they haven't changed much in millions of years. Although several chiton species are common in the rocky intertidal zone, we are looking for the largest—the gumboot chiton, which reaches nearly 6 inches in length.

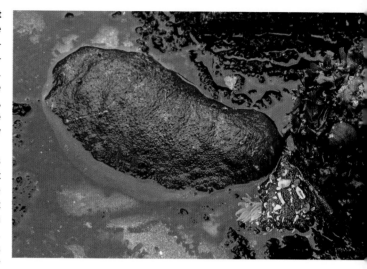

Gumboots differ from other chitons in more than just their size. While most have the plates on their dorsal side exposed, the plates on the gumboot are covered with leather-tough flesh and are brown and orange in color. It's Latin name, *Cryptochiton*, means "hidden chiton," that is, hidden under its tough skin. Gumboots roam the intertidal and subtidal zones crawling along with the aid of their large, sucker-like foot and scraping the living scum off the surface with a long rasp-like tongue called a radula. Chitons are unique among mollusk grazers in that one pair of cusps (toothlike spurs on the radula) is coated with magnetite, making it as tough as steel. Imagine your own tongue, coated with tiny metal tips. Instead of breaking food with your teeth, you would grind tiny particles off with the friction, much like sanding a block of wood with sandpaper.

Other chiton species of the Pacific Northwest Coast are relatively easy to identify because of distinctive markings. None reach the size of the gumboot. The mossy chiton features hairs and bristles around its edges. Except for the occasional barnacles attached to its plates, it resembles a balding head. The black leather chiton is sometimes called the black katy chiton. Its plates, readily visible in a row along its back, are ringed by a black leathery band. Its ability to tolerate sunlight allows it to survive higher in the intertidal zone, exposed to air and higher temperatures. ★

The largest of all chitons grazes in the intertidal by moving on its large, fleshy foot. Its Latin name, *Cryptochiton*, was given because its shell plates are hidden by its tough skin.

Other common chitons of rocky shores are the black leather chiton ◐, sometimes called black katy, and the mossy chiton ◐.

keyhole limpet

Diodora aspera

In a healthy rocky intertidal zone at low tide, every surface appears to be covered with some form of living organism, whether animal or plant. The first impression is that each organism must find space to occupy, and then hold onto that space desperately against competitors. Except for a few crabs that scatter as we pass, everything seems stuck in place. But wait, this is low tide. When the water rises, it's a signal that it's time to move. This is when the place comes alive.

Limpets are a group of mollusks that have a single conical shell and a large, suction cup–like foot. Exposed to air, they stay stuck to their spot of rocky real estate, shielded by their protective shell. But underwater, they roam, feeding on encrusting sponges and bryozoans with rasp-like teeth arranged along a ridge on their undersides. As the tide begins to ebb, limpets show remarkable navigation skills, finding their way back to their home spot to sit out the low tide. Limpets can live up to 20 years, during which time their bodies can actually erode the rock, creating a small indentation that marks home.

One of the most common limpets is the keyhole limpet, so-called because of a small circular hole at the top of its cone-shaped shell. The hole allows the limpet to excrete waste. Keyhole limpets can reach over 2 inches in length, with alternating gray and white streaks radiating away from the top of the shell.

Keyhole limpets wrap themselves in their soft mantle to evade the grip of sea star predators.

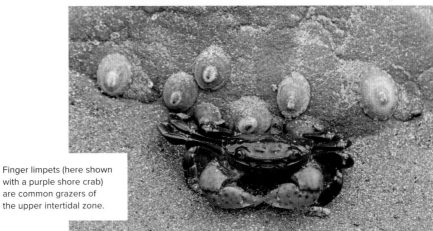

Finger limpets (here shown with a purple shore crab) are common grazers of the upper intertidal zone.

They are common in the lower reaches of the intertidal zone. The keyhole limpet shares its shell with another organism—a scale worm that actually curls into the groove between the limpet's mantle and foot, riding along and feeding on smaller worms as the limpet passes over them. The scale worm is almost a perfect match in color to the flesh of the limpet. In some experiments, scale worms removed from limpets show a preference for returning to limpets (while scale worms from other mollusks prefer their former hosts over limpets).

Keyhole limpets display a remarkable ability to foil predation from predatory sea stars. When chemical signals tell them a sea star is near, they draw the flesh of their mantle up and over their shell; the soft flesh prevents the sea star's tube feet from attaching and pulling the limpet from its hold on the rock. ★

nudibranchs or sea slugs

Nudibranchs (also known as sea slugs) are wonders of the tide pool world. Over the course of their evolution, most species of these mollusks lost their shells long ago (much like slugs in the forest) and diverged into forms that are dazzling in their color and ingenious in their life histories and adaptations.

Typically, nudibranchs are found in water—within pools or low crevices among the rocks. Sometimes they are found among seaweeds, and kept damp and protected by cover of thick marine algae or eelgrass.

Survival strategies for nudibranchs defy simple logic. For example, why would an organism that has survived for millions of years by eliminating its protective shell be such a show-off and advertise its presence with such gaudy colors?

Scientists have identified several strategies that seem to work well for nudibranchs. One is a color pattern that is disruptive or helps the animal blend in with its background. This makes the animal difficult to see or recognize, a very common strategy found throughout the plant and animal kingdoms—and one we just call camouflage.

Another ploy is to display a color pattern so obvious and so outrageous that predators can't avoid seeing and recognizing them. This is where it gets interesting: Many species of nudibranch emit chemical repellants that produce a foul taste. Several species that feed on sea anemones store the stinging cells of the anemones in their bodies and discharge them when attacked, stinging the predator. For nudibranchs that present an unpleasant flavor or an unwelcome sting, bright colors warn the predator not to mess with the otherwise helpless, slow, shell-less mouthful. That bold color pattern acts like a Mr. Yuk poison sticker, proclaiming "Don't even think about eating me." Predators learn to get the message.

Pacific Northwest nudibranchs are diverse. Over 50 species occur in our marine waters ranging in size from less than one inch to a foot in length. Identifying them confuses even some experts (here's where a good field guide comes in handy; see references).

To get started figuring out who's who, look carefully at colors and features on the animal's back. One group, the naked gill nudibranchs, are mostly light in color and have a flowerlike structure near one end of their bodies. These are the animal's gills. Look for bumps or knobs along the back. These often contain defense substances obtained from anemones or sponges—their prey. Two other groups, the bushy-backed nudibranchs and the plumed nudibranchs, are often brightly colored and display rows of elaborate branched or feather-like fingers that are extensions of their digestive systems. The tips of these fingers can be brilliant red, orange, yellow, or white. Some even appear iridescent. Near one end, look for paired tentacles—one set for feeding and one set for sensing food and possible mates.

It can take a lifetime to become a nudibranch expert, so don't worry if you can't figure out exactly which species you are looking at—simply marvel at these beautiful and complex animals sometimes known as "orchids of the sea." ★

Nudibranchs display amazing colors and diversity of forms. Plumed nudibranchs are covered with rows of feathery "fingers."

The Monterey dorid, often called a sea lemon, is one of our most common sea slugs. It belongs to a large group identified by the prominent gill "flower" at the back end of their bodies.

ochre sea star

Pisaster ochraceus

The showiest of all rocky shore ani-mals is the ochre sea star. Varying from pale yellow to bright orange and purple, these are very recognizable—and very important, ecologically. Ochre sea stars are considered keystone species, because, as predators, they shape the structure of the entire intertidal animal community.

Their favorite foods are mussels, limpets, and other mollusks. At low tide, they venture out of the water to feed on densely packed communities of the shelled animals attached to the rocks. Moving by way of thousands of tiny

Recently, ochre sea stars on the West Coast have developed a condition known as "sea star wasting syndrome," a disease that infects and attacks their tissues. Infected animals become splotchy and soft and gradually lose their legs and die. Scientists have discovered the culprit—a virus that weakens the animals' immune systems leaving them vulnerable to other infections that produce the wasting symptoms.

Complex plumbing systems govern the ochre sea star's ability to move its tube feet. The inlet valve, or madroporite, is a small white spot on the star's central disc.

tube feet, they climb over their prey, attach themselves to the shells, and pull them open with amazing strength. Once the shells are open, ochre sea stars expel their stomachs, surround the edible tissues and slowly begin to digest their prey.

However, ochre sea stars become very vulnerable if they stay out of the water too long. As visible as they are, they become easy pickings for hungry gulls. As a result, their roaming, feeding, and retreating behaviors create a distinctive visible band in intertidal areas. Exposed rocks where mussels dominate are above their comfort zone and are often dense with mussels, barnacles, and their other prey. Lower areas protected by tidal inundation typically have fewer mussels or other favorite prey animals. Sea stars should never be pried from the rocks they inhabit.

The body of the ochre sea star is a complex hydraulic system. In spite of the toughness of their exterior, they contain a lot of water. Look for a unique disc-shaped spot on the upper side of the sea star's central disc. Called a madroporite, this is an intake valve, regulating the water that enters the sea star's tissues. Once in the animal's body, water moves through several vessels in its central disc, then into the legs and delicate tube feet. The toughness of the outer skin keeps the animal from drying when exposed at low tide. ★

Sea stars come in many shapes and colors. Here, a blood star (left), sunflower star (center), and ochre sea star (right) show some of the differences.

113

purple sea urchin

Strongylocentrotus purpuratus

Three species of sea urchin are abundant in the Pacific Northwest. The most common is the purple sea urchin, easily identified by its color, rounded pin-cushion shape, and bristling display of spines.

Sea urchins are part of a group called echinoderms, Latin for "spiny-skinned." Relatives include sea stars, sea cucumbers, and sand dollars. The shell or "test" of the sea urchin is composed of ten segments, each arranged with rows of spines, tube feet, and special appendages for defense. All of these operate independently—however, the urchin moves by coordinating its spines and the tube feet.

Sea urchins are voracious consumers of seaweeds and, in large numbers, can strip the seafloor clean of algae, leaving what has been called a sea urchin barren. In areas where their predators have been removed—sea otters, for example—the entire composition of the seafloor community has been altered, with ripple effects for

Sea urchins hide themselves with bits of shell, wood, and seaweed. Tiny suckers on their tube feet cling to the concealing object.

many species. For example, when sea otters were removed from the Washington coast, sea urchin populations bounded. The urchins consumed the kelp of nearshore kelp forests, eliminating the protective habitat of many fish species. As otters were reintroduced and their range expanded, urchin populations were reduced and kelp forests and their fishes returned. The relationship between sea urchins and sea otters has been studied as an example of the importance of predation as a process that shapes entire ecosystems.

On rocky shores and in tide pools, look for purple sea urchins in the lower intertidal zone, where they get protection from gulls and other predators. Often they are clustered in cracks and crevices that make them hard to reach, or if exposed cover themselves with bits of wood, shell, and seaweed as a means of hiding. It is also common to find sea urchins tucked into holes that scientists believe the animals themselves have abraded into the rock. Purple sea urchins are very competitive and have shown aggressive behavior that includes pushing and "fencing" with their spines.

Look for an empty sea urchin test, or shell. Notice how any remaining spines are attached to the test. Look to see if the mouth area (at the bottom of the test) still has its mouth structure intact. The five-part jaw is called Aristotle's lantern because of its beautiful radial symmetry. ✯

Purple sea urchins occupy lower reaches of the intertidal zone, feeding on seaweed.

A rose among thorns: a red sea urchin stands out among its purple companions.

purple shore crab
Hemigrapsus nudus

As the tide recedes, the scurry of shore crabs is one of the most evident signs of life in the intertidal zone. Shore crabs are abundant throughout the rocky shore and tide pools and are often found in the quieter shores of estuaries.

Shore crabs are related to a large group of crabs that include land crabs found in tropical areas. One tropical species, the mangrove crab, lives in mangrove swamps and climbs the trees. Part of a large group of crabs called true crabs, all shore crabs have a wide, squarish carapace (or shell). They have agile walking legs and can move quickly along the sand and among rocks in tide pools. This quickness helps them avoid their predators—gulls, scoters, and sculpins. Once in a while, their wandering gets them into trouble: look for shell parts of unlucky crabs in partially closed sea anemones. A female shore crab, although usually less than 1½ inches

across the carapace, can produce as many as 30,000 eggs.

The purple shore crab is most common in higher-energy environments such as the outer coast. It ranges from Alaska to Mexico. It can vary in color from greenish gray to deep purple. Look for its smooth, hairless legs and for dark red or brown spots on its claws. Look closely as they feed on seaweed and small scraps of tide pool detritus—they use both claws to scoop food toward their mouths, alternating right, then left pincers. When approached, they show their feistiness by standing their ground and baring their claws. Watch out—these little guys can pinch.

Similar in size and habitat, two other shore crab species can be identified by unique markings and features. The lined shore crab is typically purple in color, with faint white or greenish lines along the broad shell of its back. The hairy or bay shore crab gets its name from tiny hairs on its legs. Its color is most often green or pale gray. ★

"Purple" shore crabs also come in color variations including pale green and gray.

rockweed

Fucus vesiculosus

The middle intertidal zone on rocky shores is often covered with a rich mat of the seaweed commonly known as rockweed. Like all brown seaweeds, rockweed plants have no roots. They attach in thick mats by a button-sized disc called a holdfast. Individual plants can reach about 20 inches in length and live for up to four years. Rockweed is easy to recognize: it is often the most abundant of all seaweeds present. It is olive-green in color, and composed of flattened branches that divide into twos, usually ending in two tips, each with a small yellowish gas-filled bubble near the end of the branch. Look closely at the blister-like sac and notice small bumps or warts. These are the reproductive parts of the plant. The bladders, which give the blades buoyancy, are filled with oxygen, carbon dioxide, and carbon monoxide, all products of the plant's respiration and photosynthesis. Pop one and see why it is sometimes called popweed.

Rockweed contains chemicals that help defend it from grazers such as limpets and snails. It can survive prolonged drying when exposed at low tides—in fact, drying helps the plant reproduce. As the air bladders dry and shrink, the eggs and sperm are forced out of the of the plant's tissue, spreading onto the nearby rocks.

Rockweed is important because it provides shelter for many invertebrates and other algae. It absorbs the shock of waves, retains moisture, and forms dense networks in which animals can forage, stay cool and wet, and avoid predators. It can be very slippery to walk on, so step carefully. Try picking through it with your hands and look for things hiding there. Look for small tubeworms, crabs, snails, and many other invertebrates. ★

The buoyant air bladders of rockweed are filled with gasses produced during the plant's respiration.

Rockweed is very susceptible to oil spills. In Alaska, rockweed communities were killed during the Exxon Valdez oil spill by oil and the hot water sprayed on it as part of the spill cleanup.

sea lettuce
Ulva fenestrata

Close your eyes and think of the greenest green you can imagine — that will get you pretty close to the green of *Ulva*, or sea lettuce. Sea lettuce resembles very thin salad lettuce. Wrinkled sheets of this brilliant, translucent seaweed line many tide pools, either attached to rocks or floating on the surface of the quiet water. The species name, *fenestrata*, comes from the holes or "windows" in the broad, thin sheets that form its blades. As its color suggests, it is a true green algae, a group of simple plants that includes over 5,000 species. Green algae range from simple filaments in ponds to complex tropical seaweeds.

Sea lettuce is an important food source in the middle and lower intertidal zones, providing nourishment for crabs, amphipods, and certain types of marine worms. Worldwide, various species of sea lettuce are known as "laver," and are eaten in soups or salads. It is very high in protein as well as vitamins and minerals (especially iron). As a defense mechanism, sea lettuce produces minute amounts of chemicals that inhibit the growth of other algae and discourage grazers like snails.

Look very carefully at the edge of a blade of sea lettuce with a magnifying glass. You may or may not be able to tell, but it is only two cells thick. When you hold it up to the light you can see its "windows."

Higher in the intertidal zone, the red algae *Porphyra* can be confused with sea lettuce. However, *Porphyra* is purple to reddish brown and often has an oil-like sheen. Like *Ulva*, *Porphyra* may have conspicuous holes in its blades, though these blades are thicker, tougher, and more resistant to drying. It is a common ingredient in Japanese cuisine, known as *nori*. ⭐

sea palm

Postelsia palmaeformis

The sea palm loves punishment. Found only on rocks exposed to fierce wave action, this seaweed takes a pounding and seemingly shakes off the waves' brutal attacks. As the name suggests, this brown algae resembles a palm tree, attached to rocks with a tough stalk up to about 2 feet tall, and topped with a mop of leaflike fronds. As waves break over the plant, frothy white foam washes off, shaking and bending the sea palm from the force. They can be found in the lower intertidal zone on the extreme edges of rocky points (look with your eyes; these are dangerous places you should probably avoid).

The sea palm is an annual, meaning that the plant grows and has a life span limited to one growing season. They appear in late winter and grow rapidly into summer. By summer's end, they die back and are gone by late autumn. Unlike their competitors on the rocks that live much longer, sea palm communities are able to withstand competitive pressure from algae, barnacles, and mussels through a very unique survival strategy. The algae's life cycle helps. When sea palms mature and

produce spores, the spores colonize the area at the base of the stalks and quickly begin to grow. As barnacles and other algae move in, young sea palms attach to them with a tough root-like knot called a holdfast and smother them. Killed or weakened, the intruders are ripped loose by wave action on the sea palm, which doesn't loosen the grip of its holdfast. Once again the rocks are stripped of competitors. But not the tiny reproductive parts of the algae called gametophytes. The sea palm is able to recolonize the bare space with the gametophytes that remain on the rock. By sacrificing some of its plants, the community itself thrives and holds onto its precious rocky real estate in order to grow and thrive for another season.

Sea palms are often torn loose and wash up on nearby beaches. Examine one closely. At the base of the stalk you will find a holdfast. See what else is attached to the holdfast—barnacles, mussels, other algae masses? If so, this sea palm contributed to its colony's survival by stripping the rock of its competitors as it was itself torn away by waves.

A thick, rubbery stalk helps the sea palm flex as surging waves pound. Found only on the most exposed rocks facing the sea, they thrive where few other organisms can.

tidepool sculpin
Oligocottus maculosus

Spot the sculpin. These small tide pool fish are perfectly colored to match their surroundings. Chances are, you will only notice them when they skitter away.

Pause for a minute before you approach the next tide pool. Look closely at the bottom and edges for small fish. You probably won't see them until you get closer; then, in a flurry, they will scatter for cover. Chances are, you are watching tidepool sculpins, small, bottom-dwelling fish with big heads and greenish or brownish saddle patches that blend with the color of sand. The first saddle, seen on the back of the head, is often very pale and wide. This coloration makes them practically invisible in their habitat, so you have to look carefully. A tidepool sculpin has sharp eyes, located on the upper of its head, letting the animal see predators and threats from all around, as well as above it. It's very likely that they saw you coming long before you saw them.

Sculpins are a large group of fishes that make ugly seem beautiful. Various species display odd horns, fringes, sharp spiny fins, and contorted faces.

Larger relatives live in deeper water and include the cabezon. In the intertidal zone, the tidepool sculpin reigns as the family's most common representative. They reach 3½ inches in length, have very blunt and broad heads, with bodies tapering sharply toward the tails. Sculpins have prominent spiny fins—the pectoral fins (on the sides, just behind the gills) look like fans and are covered with fine black spots.

Tidepool sculpins feed on algae and many small invertebrates in the intertidal zone, including amphipods and isopods, small snails, and barnacle legs. In turn, they are prey for gulls and other seabirds and larger fish that prowl the water at high tide. Individual fish show a preference for a home territory—a single tide pool or group of connected pools. Studies have shown that if fish are moved a short distance away, they will find their way back to their favorite hangouts. ★

123

Sand Beaches

From Vancouver Island to the Redwood Coast of California, sand beaches alternate with rocky headlands. Sometimes a sand beach will occupy a small cove between promontories (points of high land that jut out into the sea); elsewhere, sand beaches extend for miles. Unlike the rocky areas that remain where the ocean has eroded material, sand beaches are where the ocean has deposited it. Beach regions in the Pacific Northwest are most common along areas of broad coastal plains, in pockets between headlands, or "downstream" along ocean currents from sources of sediment, such as eroding bluffs or river entrances.

Start your explorations by looking at the sand. It's constantly in motion. Currents that run along the coast carry sand with them; when currents and wave energy weaken, it settles. Sand is also carried landward by wave energy. The sandy bottom near the shore is constantly being disturbed by the movement of water over the seafloor surface. Wave action in the surf pushes it higher up the beach. When it dries, the wind takes over and blows sand particles up the beach. In some places it blows sand hundreds of feet, even miles, forming dunes.

At first, broad, sand beaches may seem devoid of life, but the sandy intertidal zone teems with organisms. Many of them lie burrowed beneath the surface, waiting for high water so that they can feed and roam. Some, like bloodworms and mole crabs, tunnel beneath the surface, gleaning food bits from tiny cavities between the sand particles. Others, like shorebirds and gulls, look for the telltale signs of the burrowers and probe the sand to eat them.

Carried ashore by wave action and lifted into the air by wind, sand grains are constantly on the move.

Sand beaches also collect material—things living or once living, and other objects of all description. On sand beaches, we see just how far out low tide can actually be. Winter storms can lodge heavier material like logs high onto the beach; at low tide, the surf can be a quarter mile or more seaward of this debris. The last high-tide line is easy to find—look for the meandering wrack line, a continuous strand of kelp, small bits of wood and shell, pebbles, and, unfortunately, plastic debris left from the previous high tide.

Sand beaches change dramatically from season to season. In winter, when storms rage, wave energy erodes layers of sand to expose larger rocks or cobble lying underneath. In summer, typically when waves are tamer, the sand accumulates. Compare a favorite beach from summer to winter—it may look entirely different.

Sand beaches are composed of billions of loose particles of finely ground rock, moved and shaped by ocean forces, making this habitat very unstable. Because the sand beach environment is constantly in flux from wave, tide, and current, it poses great challenges to organisms living there. Sand abrasion constantly grinds exposed parts, waves tumble with great force, and the retreat of tide leaves trapped animals like crabs high and dry—and often a long way from water. And because of the instability,

The endless cadence of waves crashing on a broad strand gives a false sense of permanence to the beach landscape. Particle by particle, it is constantly changing.

very little food can actually be produced in this churning environment. Organisms that live here have to protect themselves, have ingenious ways of gathering food, and be mobile enough to move with the tides and out of the churning chaos of breakers.

Sand Beach Zones

Let's approach the sand beach the way we usually approach the shore, with the landscape of forests and fields, meadows, and towns behind us. As the familiar surroundings of the land fall away, we notice sand beneath our feet. The trees part and we find ourselves in tall beachgrass. Welcome to the dunes.

Dunes

Grassy dunes line the beach, trapping sand and sheltering hardy shore plant communities.

Dunes are products of the landward movement of sand. Like waves, which give water the power to carry sand particles, dunes are shaped by wind. Fine grains deposited on the shore by waves dry out and are blown up

the beach and beyond. Although dunes are terrestrial habitats, they are created by sand deposited by water, and create very unstable habitats that only a few organisms can survive. Plants must endure extreme drying, burial, and the constant abrasion of sand grains. Dune grasses create broad networks of root runners; plants like sand verbena often have slightly sticky surfaces that catch sand grains that may help hold the plant in place.

Dunes can cover many square miles, as along parts of the Oregon coast where they penetrate and overtake coastal forests and roads. But, except where they have been destroyed by coastal development, dunes form along most sand beach shores and create bands of low ridges separating the beach from forests, wetlands, and other coastal habitats.

Swash Zone

Emerging from the dunes, we begin to encounter logs and drift debris, cast ashore by the highest tides and strongest waves. Up high on the edge of the beach, sand is fluffy and dry. But as the waves become louder and we move closer to the water, sand becomes more compacted and damp. We encounter patches of decomposing seaweed and smaller driftwood pieces deposited not last winter, but perhaps on high tides of the past few weeks or days. It is tempting to bypass this part of the beach and make a dash for water's edge, but pause here and notice the differences between the

Sand can travel miles in the wind. Large dune fields extend along the central Oregon coastline.

The Wrack Line and Seaweed Piles

High on the sand beach, at the highest point the last high tide reached, look for seaweed, seashells, scraps of driftwood, fishing floats, feathers, bits of plastic, eelgrass, bottles, and other odds and ends. This is the wrack line, a meandering, sometimes broken line of debris that can tell us a lot about what's going on in the ocean. The wrack line gets its name in English from *wreck*, as in shipwreck or as anything that has been cast upon the shore. Seaweeds that have drifted ashore are also known as "wrack."

The wrack line is more than just a temporary stopping place for transient floating debris. It forms an important habitat of the sand beach. After intense storms, large deposits of seaweed can be found, sometimes knee deep. Sheltered from the drying effects of the sun and concealed within the damp piles you can find a host of living things like crabs seeking shelter and waiting for the tide to return, or amphipods like beach hoppers, who help the decomposition process by eating and breaking down the nutrients in the seaweed.

Piles of ocean kelp are often found littered on the beach. Two brown algae—giant kelp and bull kelp— are very common. Bull kelp resembles a long bullwhip. It has a round bulb at one end that helps it float at the water's surface, where its blades can fan out over the water. It lives in water up to 70 feet deep where there is a rocky or cobble bottom. Giant kelp is another nearshore kelp. It forms many small branches with a small bulb at the base of a broad blade. Torn away from the bottom by waves, these kelps form dense mats—floating islands that attract fish and form habitat for many species of marine invertebrates. Floating kelp mats can drift for weeks or months before they come ashore, often getting other types of debris mixed in the tangle. Pull one apart to see what's come with it. Sometimes you will find a rock attached to the end of a kelp stem. Notice the way it attaches to the stem—that rootlike mass attached to the rock is called the holdfast; the rock was its anchor.

The receding tide leaves the telltale mark of the last high tide. Look for the wrack line—a thin line of washed-up debris.

What's That Smell?
Decomposing organic material produces gasses that give off (often unpleasant) odors. Once we get past the stink, our sense

of smell can teach us a lot about how marine wildlife use their noses to find food. One chemical compound, dimethyl sulfide (DMS), is produced by bacteria found in decaying plankton. Some seabirds locate plankton-eating fish by seeking out this unique odor. To us, the smell faintly resembles boiled cabbage or cooked corn.

Seasonal storms deposit kelp on beaches, providing a windfall of recycled nutrients to the beach environment.

Something smell fishy? We often use that term to describe the faint smell of iodine and saltiness or ammonia that we associate with seafood. Fish get their fish smell from compounds called bromophenols that are present in many marine organisms that they eat. Some people have noticed that salmon, for example, that spend part of their lives in saltwater and part in freshwater, taste less "fishy" after they've been in freshwater for a while.

"Beach smell" has sometimes been used to describe a unique odor that occurs where seaweed is present. Scientists have identified chemical compounds called pheromones that are produced by some species that work as chemical signals to help seaweeds reproduce—scent texts that lead male and female parts to each other. In species that we eat, these compounds add flavor—that seaweed taste that adds to a salad or soup.

The smell of decaying flesh from a marine mammal, bird, or fish attracts all sorts of scavengers, including black bears, gulls, and eagles. Often, you will notice the stink of an animal's carcass before you see it—you've just proven you could be a successful scavenger. When you approach a carcass, remember not to touch it, but try to identify all the footprints surrounding it and notice all the signs of life that accompany the flow of nutrients from the animal back into the ecosystem.

Recycling is nature's way. A longnose skate, its "wings" already eaten, lies on the beach.

world of forest and dune and the water's edge. Turn over a pile of seaweed. Immediately, beach hoppers, feeding on the decomposing algae, leap and bounce and scatter to find cover. What other kinds of debris can you find? Feathers? Bits of plastic?

Wet Sand

The wet sand represents the true intertidal zone of the sand beach. This is the area that was washed on the last high tide, exposed at low tide, and will probably be washed on the next high tide. Look for tracks—large webbed gull tracks or multitudes of smaller bird footprints, from sandpipers. Other signs of bird activity include disturbed sand, where sandpipers and

The ocean carries, and gives up, its flotsam and jetsam. Marine debris has become one of the ocean's big problems.

other sand foragers have pecked and probed the sand in search of food. Look for variations in sand patterns. Finer sand is often deposited in patterns that reveal water runoff: triangles and branching rivulets (small streams). Look for the holes of burrowing creatures—beach hoppers and worms. Try digging up a handful or shovel-full of the sand. You'll be surprised at what you find in what looks like a deserted beach. Where the water runs up the beach in thin, bubble-edged layers, look for mole crabs, their legs and antennae sticking above the sand and creating V-shaped wakes as the water moves around them.

The Surf Environment

The surf zone is the beach's most turbulent environment. Here, sand is constantly being lifted and sorted by the wave wash and the water is dirty with suspended particles. This is also the most oxygenated water on the beach, so don't be surprised to find fish like surf perch and skates thriving in this environment,

When the tide is out, the table is set—for birds and other foragers that know what lies beneath the surface.

Thin sheets of water create patterns in the sand. Erosion, on a microscale, is always moving sand particles.

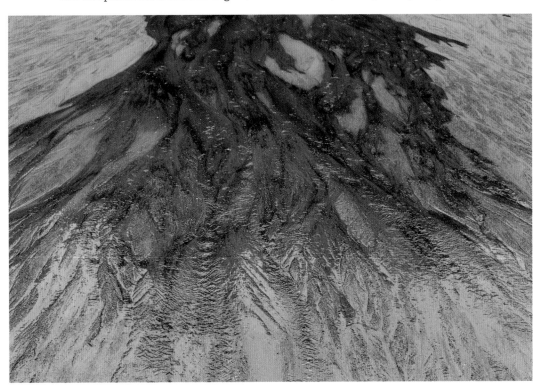

Just beyond the foam, ocean worlds lie unseen. The shallows are alive with fish and clams and other animals that can withstand the dynamic conditions.

Shorebird Mayhem

Shorebirds of the beach present one of the most dynamic wildlife spectacles we see—over 80 species migrate through or breed within our region.

To really get to know shorebirds by sight takes a long time—learning the names, habits, and field marks vexes even advanced birders. To make matters worse, a bird that is black and white during its breeding season may be all white the rest of the year and mottled during it's molting or feather-changing season. That's a lot to remember—even the best birders often forget. Identifying shorebirds requires good binoculars, a good bird field guide, and an uncanny eye for detail.

What's important to remember for us beginning naturalists is to look for obvious differences in size and beak length among different species of shorebirds. This is our best clue for identifying them, what they eat, and how they use the sand beach environment. Because shorebirds are a large group of hungry foragers, each species competes with every other species for limited food resources. Each has developed unique adaptations in order to assure success and survival over time. Some feed by seeing their food, some by feeling or hearing. Those with long probelike bills poke deep into the sand; others, with short, stubby beaks, peck at the surface for insects and small bits of food. Birders often divide shorebirds into two groups: the probers and the gleaners. Probers feed on invertebrates that are burrowed into the sand. Their bills are often long, sometimes pointed downward or even curved. They feed on shellfish like clams and beach worms whose movements they sense by feel. Gleaners scurry over the surface, seeing and pecking on beach insects and other invertebrates.

Probing strategies are used by small sandpipers like the western sandpiper and larger sandpipers like the willet and yellowlegs. Gleaners include sanderlings and plovers. Plovers provide good examples of visual hunting. They stand upright, visually scanning for food, sometimes vibrating the ground slightly. Once they spot their prey, they stoop to pluck it into their bills.

in spite of the rough and tumble treatment they are getting. They will be searching for their favorite foods, including razor clam necks, sand shrimp, and mole crabs.

Wash-Ups and Odds and Ends

Sand beaches collect. The currents that deliver sand to a sand beach shoreline bring all sorts of other things as well, from whole ships, to dead or stranded whales, to glass fishing floats, to large and small bits of plastic. Maybe this is why beachcombing is so popular—you never know what you will find when the tide recedes.

Bird "Wrecks"

Winter storms, oil spills, and blooms of toxic algae can be devastating to seabirds on the open ocean. Occasionally, large groups of birds are weakened or killed by these conditions and wash up on beaches. Pacific Northwest beaches are routinely monitored by volunteer citizen scientists who identify beached bird remains and provide data to researchers. Casual beachcombers who find dead birds may notice colorful plastic zip ties attached to bird carcasses. This signifies that the bird has been recorded and shouldn't be disturbed. Beach-cast birds give us an opportunity to look more closely at birds that we normally can't see from land. Look at the variations among bird families—their beaks and feet can help us identify even badly decomposed remains and reveal the many physical adaptations that help them survive on the open ocean.

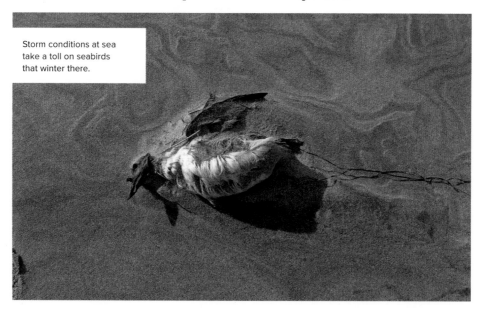

Storm conditions at sea take a toll on seabirds that winter there.

Marine Mammals

Chances are, you will encounter dead whales, porpoises, seals, and sea lions on Pacific Northwest beaches. Most often, these animals have died of natural causes. Occasionally, however, death has been caused by humans: a whale struck by a ship, a sea lion shot by someone, or a seal entangled in rope or other marine debris. Their presence is usually betrayed by their powerful odor.

It's important not to touch marine mammal carcasses. But a beached carcass gives us a chance to see the physical features of marine mammals. On large whales, study the baleen or large features like fins, flukes, and other parts. On sea lions, look for the powerful canine teeth that reveal their ancestral links to land carnivores.

Encountering a live, but stricken, marine mammal can be a powerful emotional experience. None of us likes to see animals suffer. There is little any of us can—or should—do to help. Marine mammal rescue is highly dangerous, and requires special authorities, skills, and equipment. Injured or sick animals can be very unpredictable and dangerous. Besides being big, and having large teeth, they can transmit animal diseases. In some cases, animals may look sick, but just need a secluded beach, without predators, to rest and recuperate. Female northern elephant seals, for example, migrate through our waters and come ashore for one or more

The "abandoned" baby seal often isn't—Mom may just be off finding food. Never approach or handle seals or sea lions resting on the beach.

weeks to molt (or shed) their hair. They look like they are diseased and dying, when they actually just need to rest in the sand and be free of the harassment of pets and people. Always report injured or ill marine mammals at the nearest ranger station. Throughout the Pacific Northwest, official marine mammal stranding networks are in place to respond, gather data, assist where possible, and enforce the laws that protect the animals.

There's also the phenomenon of the "abandoned baby seal." Each spring and summer baby harbor seals appear on our beaches—at about the same time that we humans start to enjoy the same beaches for our recreation. And each year, scores of baby seals are removed by onlookers who think the babies need to be rescued. Those that are removed rarely survive for long or make it back into the wild. It is normal behavior for mothers of newborns to leave them on the beach while Mom forages for food. When occasionally the mothers do abandon their young and often, it's because humans have touched or moved the infant. As with sick or dying animals, notify local authorities of the presence of a baby seal. In some communities, volunteers will monitor the animal from a safe distance, keeping people and pets from harassing the little tyke.

Marine Debris

Many of our beaches have begun to look like landfills. It's that simple. Even the most remote beaches on the planet have acquired the detritus of civilization, often in the form of plastics that will, unfortunately, persist in the ecosystem for decades or centuries.

What is most disheartening about beach debris is that it reflects human callousness toward the ocean. Decades' worth of garbage has made its way into marine ecosystems, either thrown overboard at sea or washed down through our watersheds. Events like storms and tsunamis contribute to the debris, but the majority of marine debris is the product of human carelessness.

In addition to being unsightly, marine debris is a threat to the health of marine wildlife and people. Nets and plastic rings ensnare and strangle many forms of marine wildlife. Some objects resemble food and are consumed by seabirds, sea turtles, and fish. Large pieces of Styrofoam often display bite marks where they've been chewed by animals.

The ocean is littered with human trash. A large part of the central Pacific Ocean is known as the "Garbage Patch" because of vast areas of circulating debris. Only when it washes ashore do we notice it. It's more than an eyesore, much of it endangers wildlife or contains toxic materials.

Cultural and Historic Objects

A beach eroded by a strong winter storm can sometimes be a window to the past. Castaway parts of shipwrecks and Native American cultural artifacts occasionally show up on our beaches. However, removing them as souvenirs is like tearing a chapter from a book—out of place, they don't give historians and archaeologists a chance to study the whole story, the context. Responsible beachcombers have made important contributions to shipwreck and prehistoric archaeology. It was an observant hiker who noticed—and reported—artifacts eroding from the beach at Ozette, Washington. That discovery led to one of the most important archaeological finds in the Pacific Northwest—whole houses preserved in mud, with thousands of artifacts now preserved and displayed at the Makah Museum in Neah Bay. If you find objects that appear to have historic or archaeological significance, take pictures, note an accurate location and contact park rangers or that state's office of historic preservation or archaeology as soon as possible.

The rugged Pacific Northwest Coast has taken its share of ships. Remains, like the anchor of the bark Austria, wrecked in 1887, are historically significant and should not be disturbed or removed.

beachgrass

Ammophila arenaria

European beachgrass was introduced as a way of stabilizing dunes. Its knotted root system reaches deep into the sand, blocking its movement. Many areas "stabilized" by the exotic grass were home to rare native plants, insects, and birds whose habitats the grass destroyed.

The most conspicuous plants on Pacific Northwest sand dunes are grasses—waist-high and arched as they bend in the wind. Grasses of the dunes are important for stabilizing dunes. Their root systems extend great distances beneath the sand, acting as fibers that reinforce the structure of dunes. They tolerate salt, both in the air and in the water that penetrates the dunes.

Unfortunately, most grasses covering Pacific Northwest coastal dunes are nonnative and very aggressive. Beachgrass was introduced from Europe over 100 years ago as a way to slow the movement of sand where human development, like roads and houses, were at risk. Nearly everywhere, it succeeded, even in places where no harm would come from sand movement and dune migration. Unfortunately, its introduction and spread permanently altered the natural processes of dune formation and ecology and had impacts on dune wetlands, plant communities, and entire succession processes.

Prior to dune stabilization efforts, blowing sand formed low foredunes, the ones closest to the beach, and native grasses formed clumps with gaps. Small hummocks of plants were distributed through the dune community allowing dunes to move among them. Solid communities of invasive beachgrass created higher foredunes and denser stands of grass, preventing sand transport inland. With the exotic grass, the foredune is often continuous, creating a wall that prevents the landward movement of sand. This may seem desirable in developed areas, but in areas managed as natural communities, or that are habitat for threatened or endangered species, natural dune processes are critical. In native dune habitats, the diversity of the plant and communities is higher. Wildlife move more easily between forest and beach. Dune processes, always dynamic, contribute to a mosaic of habitats. ⭐

beachgrass

Native coastal dune communities are some of the rarest in the Pacific Northwest. From grazing and agriculture during the settlement period of the coast, to urbanization and development of more recent times, much of the native coastal dune community has been lost. Restoration efforts are underway in some places, but the assault of exotic plants on native coastal dune habitat has taken its toll.

Dune ecology is a study of processes that begin in the ocean and reach far into the terrestrial environment, shaping the land and the forest communities of the coastal region.

beach hopper
Megalorchestia californiana

Reach down with your hand and flip over a pile of seaweed that is decomposing on the beach. If you are lucky, out will jump a beach hopper. If you are really lucky, a shower of them will hop out. Sometimes called sand fleas, they are not related to fleas. In fact, they aren't even insects. They are amphipod crustaceans that live burrowed in fine beach sand and feed on dead and decaying seaweed. So don't worry, they won't bite.

Two species are common on our beaches. The California beach hopper can be recognized by the bright orange section at the base of its antennae. They can reach just over an inch in length. The other, simply called beach hopper, is smaller and is a uniform gray in color. During the day, beach hoppers burrow in the sand or beneath seaweed piles seeking shelter from predators and to stay cool and moist. At night, they roam the sand surface, hopping around in search of decaying seaweed and other organic material. Beach hoppers are really terrestrial animals. They stay out of the water—otherwise they'll drown.

Male beach hoppers are very competitive. They will often fight over desirable burrows, food, and for access to female beach hoppers. This aggressive behavior is often costly to animals, who risk their lives, injury, or being displaced from good habitat if they lose. Some ecologists think that fighting is common among male beach hoppers

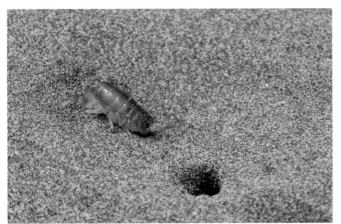

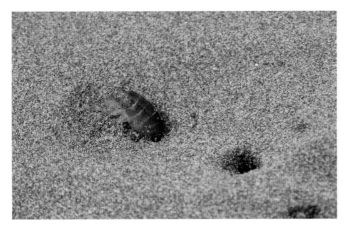

Going, going. . . . A beach hopper retreats quickly into the protection of the sand.

because it is easier for one beach hopper to claim another's burrow than to dig one for himself.

Beach hoppers play an important ecological role on the beach. Vast in numbers, they recycle large amounts of decaying seaweed, breaking it into minute bits and assisting in the decaying process. They are, in turn, an important food source for beetles and shorebirds. Raccoons and moles are even known to feed on larger specimens.

How far can a beach hopper hop? Beach hoppers have very powerful jumping legs and can launch themselves into the air, jumping as much as ten times their body length. The record for a human doing a broad jump from a standing position is just over 12 feet. That's just about two times an adult male's height. How tall are you? How far could you jump if you had legs as strong as a beach hopper? ★

bloodworm

Euzonus mucronatus

Marine worms come in all shapes and sizes and, as a large group of marine invertebrates, are extremely important in beach and mudflat food chains. On the high-energy sand beach, the most common worm is the bloodworm.

Keep a sharp eye out in the mid-tide section of the beach for spots where the smooth sand has a pitted texture comprised of many tiny holes. These patches are usually in the same section of the beach, running parallel to the water. Dig in a few inches with your hands and you are likely to find a cluster of bloodworms, stretchy, stringy, beet-red segmented worms that live in the sand. When you find some, look closely at their bodies—the head is spade-shaped and separated from its thorax by a necklike constriction. The thorax ends at the mantle. Moving down the body, notice that it tapers toward its rear end.

Bloodworms are to the beach what earthworms are to your garden. They wiggle among the sand particles, eating organic material that clings to the sand particles and fills the space between. Bloodworms actually swallow whole sand grains and let their digestive system absorb whatever nutrients cling to the sand. They may be the most abundant organism of the wet intertidal sand. They are very picky, however, about where they locate. They concentrate in bands, where the moisture and oxygen levels are just right. They cluster in groups that may number over a hundred but occupy an area that is just inches wide.

In the sand, they move by stretching and contracting, just like earthworms, sometimes reaching a foot in length. Pulled from the sand, they shrink to just a few inches long. Don't worry about biting; they get their name from their color—not from eating blood. ★

Bloodworms ingest sand grains and extract minute particles of food that cling to them. Only inches long when they contract, they can stretch out up to a foot long.

by-the-wind sailor
Velella velella

This small, bluish animal is about the size of an oval 50-cent piece. They often arrive by the thousands in spring or early summer, stranding on the sand beach, and creating stink and spectacle for beach watchers. What you see as a single individual is actually a colony of individual specialized polyps, all doing their part for survival. Some feed, others form the stinging cells, and some are the reproductive parts. Put them all together and you have a small, translucent sail-powered raft that roams the open sea, buoyed by a flat, gas-filled bladder.

By-the-wind sailors, or *Velella*, are small jellyfish-like animals that drift over the wide ocean. Each year, they wash up on the shore, sometimes in great numbers.

A stiff, thin, cellophane-like membrane stands upright, forming a three-sided sail that catches the wind. On the underside, small tentacles dangle just beneath the surface, capturing zooplankton (tiny drifting animals or animal larvae), fish eggs, and other food. Driven over the ocean by breezes, they sail our temperate ocean at a 45-degree angle to the wind. In light to moderate wind, this keeps them well out to sea. In heavy winds, however, they lose control of their orientation and drift with the wind, often toward shore.

Seeing a broad beach littered with by-the-wind sailors can seem alarming—how can the species survive such die-offs? They survive because those that drift ashore are a minute fraction of this open ocean jelly's population.

Like other jellies, by-the-wind sailors have stinging cells that they use to immobilize their prey. The toxins they release, however, are not strong enough to give you a painful sting, though it's still not a good idea to rub your eyes after touching a by-the-wind sailor. Give your hands a good soapy scrub. ⭐

Worldwide, populations of jellyfish appear to be on the rise. Scientists point to warming oceans and overfishing as factors. Jellies may be increasing because of the ripple effects of the loss of major predators like swordfish and sharks, compounded by changing physical and chemical conditions in the world ocean. Because they are well adapted to warm water and feed low on the food chain, they may fare well in the changing ocean of the future.

mole crab
Emerita analoga

In the rough and tumble world of the sand beach, the mole crab (sometimes called sand crab), is perfectly adapted to its environment. Roughly the size and shape of an olive and protected by a tough shell, the mole crab has powerful digging legs and can quickly burrow backward into the sand. Unlike other crabs, it lacks claws. It is the ultimate surfer, riding the waves that pound into the beach and relocating as the tide rises and falls to stay in the turbulence of the swash zone where food is plentiful. With its rear end planted in the sand, it strokes the water with hairy antennae, catching food particles that it wipes into its mouth. If the wave pulls the crab from the sand, it tumbles, recovers its bearings, and swims back to the sand, burrowing in again.

Although they range from California to British Columbia, their appearance in Oregon and Washington appears to coincide with El Niño events. Large reproducing populations occur in California; populations in Oregon and Washington are stocked by larvae that drift northward. Look for them in the swash zone, or sand in the shallow run-up of waves. By digging with your hands just a few inches beneath the surface, you should find them in abundance—if warm southern waters have brought them north.

Like other crabs, they gradually outgrow their shells. The cast-off shells are often found in the drift line, or littered on the beach. This should be your clue that they are present on your particular beach. Females are larger than males, sometimes reaching 2 inches in length, compared to ¾ inch for males. Females incubate bright egg masses beneath a flap on their underside called a telson (or sometimes called a digger).

If you find a mole crab, you can distinguish females from males by the

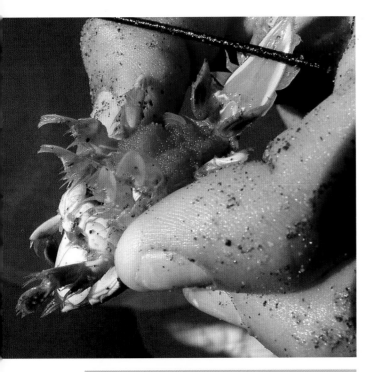

presence of eggs or specialized legs under the telson. As many as 45,000 eggs may be present. The female will incubate the eggs for about a month, before they release and roam in the ocean as larvae. In the ocean, the larvae drift, feeding on plankton for four or five months. During this time, they pass through several stages as larvae. Young "recruits" eventually settle into suitable beach habitat. ⭐

A female mole crab reveals her eggs. Larval mole crabs travel along the California Current, settling on Northwest beaches during El Niño events. Conditions in the North don't favor self-sustaining populations.

The importance of mole crabs in the food chain is recognized by many scientists who monitor for the presence of pollutants, like DDT (a now-banned pesticide). They also study mole crabs to detect domoic acid, a naturally occurring toxin produced by plankton. Although domoic acid is harmless to mole crabs, it can be lethal to predators that consume large quantities of the crustacean when the toxic plankton blooms in the ocean.

Mole crabs are perfectly suited to life in the sand. With pop-up eyes and specialized digging and feeding tools, they endure a rough and tumble life in the surf zone.

olive snail
Olivella biplicata

The olive snail's range is widespread—from Alaska to Baja California—but it requires the sand beach as its habitat. Equipped with a long siphon for exchanging water and a strong, wedge-shaped foot for digging, it survives the rigors of the sandy intertidal zone by being compact and football-shaped. The inch-long shells are light brownish to light gray, and often rimmed with purple along the shell's spiral and inner surface. It is an opportunistic feeder, eating kelp and fine particles of organic debris. Common predators of the olive snail include gulls, moon snails, octopus, and sea stars.

Olive snails are most active at night, burrowing just beneath the surface of the sand as they feed and roam. Their tracks can be identified as long, winding furrows that rise above the surrounding sand. Often, the form of the snail itself is revealed as a lump at the end of its track line. Males are said to locate females by finding a track and following it to a female snail. Once located, they attach to the female and mating occurs. Fertilized eggs are tiny—about $\frac{1}{64}$ of an inch in size—and are attached to small rocks. Olive snails may live to be eight to fifteen years old.

Sometimes, olive snails occur in large congregations. Look for patches of conspicuous lumps in disturbed wet sand near water's edge. Individual snails may be visible just poking out of shallow holes in the sand. Look carefully for the siphon. When alarmed, olive snails are fast diggers and can escape quickly. ★

Eating aside, perhaps the most prized of sand beach mollusks is the olive snail. Traditionally gathered by coastal tribes and transformed into bead necklaces, bracelets, and other regalia, olive shells represent beauty and abundance. Olive shell necklaces have been found in eastern Washington archaeology digs dating back over 9,000 years. The value and cultural importance of olive snails continues today.

Olive snails are found in the sand intertidal at a higher stage than razor clams. The small snail plows its way through the sand, eating smaller organisms. They sometimes appear in swarms, large groups just beneath the wet sand.

Long prized for trade and dance regalia, olive shell beads are an important ceremonial resource for Native Americans and First Nations people. On reservation beaches, gathering is regulated by custom. Outsiders should never harvest them.

razor clam
Siliqua patula

Ask anybody who lives in a Pacific Northwest beach community what draws the most visitors to the region's sand beaches, and you'll get the same answer: it's the razor clam. Yes, a lowly mollusk. Local economies thrive when razor clam populations thrive. Hoards are drawn to the beaches at all hours when there's a good low tide for clamming. Roads and parking lots are jammed. Beaches are covered with people with shovels and clam "guns" (handled tubes pushed into the sand). On good clam tides, a thousand or more clam diggers with lanterns and gawky rain gear can be seen at the edge of the tide line in search of what many consider the king of all clams.

On a good low tide, go to the edge of the water, where the water washes over the sand just inches deep. Look for razor clam "shows," holes left where the clam has just pulled in its siphon. Shows are what eagle-eyed clam diggers are looking for. When they find one, experienced diggers move quickly, shoveling rapidly or pushing their clam gun into the wet sand. They'd better move fast or that clam's going to get away!

The clam's range is from central California to Alaska. In Alaska's colder waters, the clam grows slowly and can live for as long as 15 years, reaching 11 inches in length. It reaches about 6 inches in length in the Pacific Northwest.

The razor clam is ideally suited to the sand beach environment and all its rigors. It's thin profile and amazing digging ability allow it to burrow quickly—disappearing into the wet sand in seconds. It's shell is thin and golden in color. It prefers the wet sand environment; low tides of between 3 and −2 feet are when they are most visible—and easiest to harvest. The razor clam feeds primarily on diatoms, simple planktonic organisms, drawn in with seawater through its elongated siphon. Two tubes—one carrying seawater in, and one out—let it suck in nutrient-rich water that is filtered over its gills. Small bits of food are passed to its digestive system. Larger bits (like sand particles) are expelled. The clam digs with a powerful foot—its "digger"—which is prized as the muscular food portion of the clam.

Razor clams are an important food source for other organisms. Their protruding siphons are nibbled by surf perch and other nearshore fishes. Other predators include Dungeness crab and shorebirds. Surf fishermen often use clam siphons as bait. ★

Because they are filter feeders, razor clams can accumulate toxic plankton and have been known to contain domoic acid. Razor clam populations are closely monitored for toxins, as well as to determine if the populations are strong enough to meet the demand for recreational clam diggers. Be sure to check with the local department of fish and wildlife for clam season information—for health warnings as well as for the times you can harvest legally.

redtail surf perch

Amphistichus rhodoterus

Surf perch live in the tumbling water at the shore's edge. Prized by saltwater anglers, surf perches form large schools that patrol the channels just beneath the breakers, gleaning mole crabs, shrimp, and other prey that washes off the beach, snipping off clam necks sticking out of the sand, and consuming just about anything else they find appetizing. Predators of surf perches include seals and sea lions, brown pelicans, terns, and larger nearshore fishes.

The most commonly fished surf perch in the Pacific Northwest is the redtail surf perch, which can reach 16 inches in length and weigh as much as 4 pounds. As a group, surf perches live only in the North Pacific. Redtail surf perches are found from about Monterey Bay to Vancouver Island.

The fish resemble freshwater perches—oval in shape with flattened sides and a forked tail. The fish has bright reddish fins (and tail) and vertical stripes along its sides. The dorsal fin (along its back) has spiny rays toward the front and soft rays toward the tail. You probably won't see one in the wild, but chances are an avid surf fisher will be happy to show off their catch.

Surf perch bear their young alive. Males may compete with each other to mate with a female. After the female is fertilized, the eggs grow inside her body for six to eight months. Typically, a litter is composed of three to ten young. Surf perch can live up to 14 years. They are very social, schooling in large groups, and have been observed being dominated by a larger surf perch that keeps the school together—the schoolmaster? ★

sand dollar

Dendraster excentricus

Of the world's sand dollars, Pacific Northwest sand dollars are unique in several ways. First is their name—*Dendraster excentricus*—which is literally translated as "tree" (dendro), "star" (aster), "off-center" (excentricus.) Our sand dollars are nearly circular, reaching about 3 inches in diameter. Their top sides are etched with a five-pointed petal- or leaflike pattern, located off-center of the animal's disc-like exoskeleton. On the bottom or "oral" side, they feature a pattern of grooves, radiating out from a central mouth opening. "Top" and "bottom" aren't really accurate, however, for living animals. We usually see them that way after they have died, when what we are holding is the animal's bleached white skeleton, or "test."

Alive and thriving, sand dollars sit upright, partially anchored on edge and embedded in the sand. This also sets them apart from their worldwide

The bleached sand dollars we see on the beach are the skeletons, or "tests," of the animal. Like its sea urchin relatives, living sand dollars are covered with spines—short hairlike feet with specialized functions for feeding and movement.

relatives, most of which feed by crawling along the seabed and gleaning food bits from the sand or silt. Large colonies of our sand dollars line up, facing the waves and capturing bits of food debris suspended in the turbulence.

Living sand dollars are covered with a lush purple-gray, fuzzy coat of short spines. Minute "feet" spines are found among their fuzz on their oral sides, allowing them to crawl. Special tube feet are found in their petal pattern, specialized for respiration. In very turbulent water, they flatten themselves against the seabed.

The five-part symmetry and spines are characteristic of other familiar intertidal animals, including sea urchins and sea stars. Another feature common among these spiny invertebrates is a five-part jawlike mouth, just visible in the oral opening. ★

western sandpiper

Calidris mauri

Imagine for a moment that you weigh exactly one ounce, and each year you have to fly—under your own power—from Mexico to northwest Alaska and back again. You can't take any food with you. There had better be lots of rest stops along the way, with plenty of food for refueling. This is the plight of the western sandpiper. Fortunately, mudflats and beaches in the Pacific Northwest are evenly scattered along the way.

The peak western sandpiper migration season begins in April, when they leave their wintering range in Mexico and Central America. On the breeding grounds in Alaska, females lay four spotted eggs. When they hatch, the young feed voraciously on tundra insects. Adults begin their southward migration in July. Vast flocks of younger birds depart in August. During both migrations, multitudes of western sandpipers move along the coast as if it were an interstate—estuary mudflats and sand beaches are their truck stops along the thousand-plus-mile routes. On Pacific Northwest beaches we see the western sandpiper in large flocks. They scurry along the water's edge making a distinctive, high-pitched "jeet" sound. Suddenly, as one, they rise into flight, like a bright cloud flashing in the sunlight as they turn.

Western sandpipers are part of a large group of shorebirds that are generally known as sandpipers. Species identification is often difficult. They are very small, with bills that point slightly downward. We usually see them in their nonbreeding plumage, with a lightly speckled, pale breast. Legs are black. ★

yellow sand verbena

Abronia latifolia

The showy beach and dune plant yellow sand verbena, grows in low, spreading mats, often on the back sides of dunes and along the upper parts of the beach, tucked among logs, low grasses, and other beach plants like beach pea and sea rocket.

When it blooms in late spring and summer, sand verbena sends up a bright ball of yellow flowers, each individual floret looking like a tiny trumpet. Get close to see if you can catch its fragrance. Sand verbena leaves are round and low to the ground. The leaves are well adapted to the drying effects of the sun and the unstable sand environment. A thick, waxy outer layer of cells retains water in the leaf tissues. A tacky film on their surface catches sand grains. Sand verbena is anchored in the sand by a thick, woody knot of roots, which are often exposed where the sand has blown away.

After the blooms have matured, they form into bizarrely shaped seedheads. These too are sticky and are soon partly buried in sand—a perfect way to ensure a good seedbed for germination and sprouting. ★

Present in Oregon and California, pink sand verbena was thought to be extinct on Vancouver Island. The discovery of a few plants has led to a recovery effort in Pacific Rim National Park Reserve.

Pink sand verbena is a close relative of yellow sand verbena. Considered rare, populations in California are associated with dune communities. In Oregon, pink sand verbena lives on the upper sand beach. It is considered extinct in Washington, but is being restored in Pacific Rim National Park Reserve on Vancouver Island. The plant was thought to have vanished there too, but a few plants were discovered in 2000 and 2001. Researchers spent several years collecting seeds and learning how to propagate them. As a result, small populations were reestablished at several locations within the park—a conservation success story.

Nearshore

At just under 6 feet tall, standing on a beach with my toes just getting wet, the distance I can see to the horizon on a clear day is about three miles. Standing on a bluff overlooking the ocean, I can see farther. While, technically, "nearshore" may extend as far as the edge of the continental shelf, for our purposes the nearshore waters are those we can see. This is where the worlds of land, air, and sea all come together. Whales rise to breathe and seabirds wheel in flight over the wave crests or dabble on the water's surface. Kelp beds, anchored to a shallow rocky bottom, float on the swells. That lip of water is the boundary to our casual investigation, but our gaze extends beyond and is often rewarded by sights and sounds—the momentary clues to unseen life in the ocean, its depths and its breadth, and most of all, the vitality of its living systems, invisible to us.

Nearshore waters are among the ocean's most productive. Currents provide mixing, bringing nutrients into shallows where sunlight reaches through the water column. Animals that live part-time on land, such as cliff-nesting seabirds or river otters, pass back and forth between the water world, where they feed, and land, where they find shelter and breed. Marine mammals that, like us, must breathe air through nostrils and into lungs, surface to catch their breath, even though the rest of their bodies have adapted fully to aquatic life. Seals come ashore to shed their skin, ducks to find shelter, flightless as their feathers molt. Predators, like orcas and great white sharks, sometimes prowl the shallows, using the sloping bottom to trap their prey. Fishes, like herring and smelt, spawn in beach gravel.

It's best to observe the visible nearshore from some height. A cape or headland will help. For every additional 10 feet of elevation ("height of eye"), a little less than one more mile becomes visible. And downward viewing angles reduce glare and allow us to see not just what pops out of the surface of the water, but what's just beneath it. A high vantage lets us see over swells and waves, so we can gauge the full extent of a kelp bed or raft of seabirds.

Spotting scopes and binoculars definitely help. The difference between "that speck in line with that rock" and "that sea otter washing its face" is often just measured as a few fractions of an inch of precision-ground glass—lenses that magnify our own eyesight. And the distances that telescope, binocular, and camera lenses keep between us and what we are observing can mean we are not disturbing our quarry—that what we are seeing is truly "natural" behavior and is not affected by our presence.

Once in a while, we get the opportunity to visit the nearshore waters by boat—kayaking, out fishing, or on a whale- or bird-watching trip. These are rare opportunities to get up close and personal with the nearshore environment. If you aren't prone to seasickness, the movements of wave and swell are mesmerizing, and the feel of wave spray invigorating. On whale-watch trips, you can smell their fetid breath and see the glossy "footprints" left on the surface by the movement of their flukes. You can watch seabirds sitting on the water, or observe the graceful flight of shearwaters as they skim the wave tops. Watch for feeding frenzies of gulls and other birds as they forage for bait fish that ball up just below the surface. Underwater, those fish are probably also being pursued by dogfish or other predators. Look at rip lines, where currents converge. Here, plankton often concentrate and feeding activity above and below the surface is intense.

Always remember, however, to give marine mammals and nesting seabirds plenty of space—federal laws forbid their harassment. Conscientious professional wildlife-watching guides and boat operators will keep their distances. These are among our most imperiled wildlife species—they deserve respect.

Sweeping views of the ocean sometimes yield surprises. A migrating gray whale passes through common murres at Yaquina Head, a perfect vantage point for nearshore wildlife watching.

brown pelican
Pelecanus occidentalis

In the 1950s and 60s, when the pesticide DDT was used indiscriminately, the toxic effects of the chemical moved through the food chain and concentrated in the pelicans, the top predators of schooling fishes. This caused eggs to form with shells that were too fragile to withstand the weight of the brooding adults. As eggs collapsed, so did the pelican population.

Since laws were passed banning DDT, brown pelicans have bounced back and are considered stable now. Brown pelican sightings in the Pacific Northwest increased dramatically in the 1980s. Birds missing from the coastal landscape reappeared during the 1982 El Niño event, when warmer waters changed fish population patterns all along the West Coast. As the fish moved, so did the pelicans. Since then, they have become regular seasonal visitors.

Once endangered almost to the point of extinction, the brown pelican graces our coast during summer months. Long strands of them course over the breakers; congregations roost on jetties, beaches and rocks. Their large size and oversized bill make them immediately recognizable. They have massive gray-brown bodies, brown necks, whitish heads and a bright red gular pouch that folds neatly inside their lower jaw.

Brown pelicans are plunge feeders. They hunt fish from aloft, wheel in the air, collapse their wings, and twist to one side to crash through the water's surface, often stunning fish as they strike them. They then gulp up water—and fish—straining the fish bits as they expel the water from their capacious pouch. Often during their showy feeding sessions, pelicans will attract gulls and terns that try to steal their catch.

Brown pelicans breed in large colonies. On the West Coast, breeding range extends from southern California to Ecuador. Nests are made of sticks and grass, sometimes in trees, but often on the ground on protected, offshore islands. The eggs are incubated within the webbed folds of the adults' feet—essentially the parents stand on the eggs to hatch them.

bull kelp
Nereocystis luetkeana

Look along rocky Pacific Northwest shores where the water isn't deeper than 60–80 feet and notice the lush forests of olive-green kelp fan out and sway with the waves. What we see from land or from a boat is a floating canopy, supported by hollow stems and buoyant bulbs. But what's underneath is as lush as any rain forest. Beneath the surface, kelp forests teem with fishes and invertebrates and—along the Washington coast—sea otters.

Kelp forests are to the coastal waters what conifer forests are to the coastal slopes—productive communities and complex structures that sustain many life forms. Bull kelp is one of the fastest-growing plants known, growing almost 6 inches a day or up

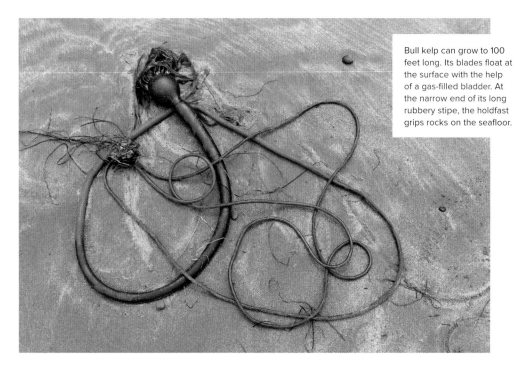

Bull kelp can grow to 100 feet long. Its blades float at the surface with the help of a gas-filled bladder. At the narrow end of its long rubbery stipe, the holdfast grips rocks on the seafloor.

to 100 feet in a single growing season. And even though bull kelp dies off after one season, tangled mats of kelp continue to drift in the ocean, forming floating islands that shelter fish, invertebrates, and their larvae.

The bull kelp plant is anchored to rocks by a rootlike wad known as a holdfast. Its tapered hollow stem—or stipe—ends in a bulb. The bulb and stipe are filled with a combination of oxygen, nitrogen, and carbon monoxide that keep it afloat. Broad garlands of leaflike blades are attached to the bulb and fan out over the water surface. ★

The ecological importance of kelp forests is profound. Studies of food chain interactions in kelp forests reveal the importance of sea otters as predators of sea urchins, which eat kelp and can rapidly denude an area of kelp. When kept in check by sea otters, kelp forests thrive—along with fish and invertebrate populations. When sea otters are not present, urchins can rapidly consume kelp, creating what are called sea urchin barrens. Overall balance is maintained by healthy populations all around. Kelp is food for urchins; urchins are food for otters; and otters—and scores of other species—depend on the kelp forest for shelter.

California gray whale

Eschrichtius robustus

On their way to the Bering and Chuk- chi seas, gray whales make their spring passage close enough to land that we can see them spouting, fluking, spy-hopping (poking their heads out of water), and breaching from headlands, capes, and even beaches. Your travel distance to the coast is nothing compared to their annual journey of up to 13,000 miles—thought to be the longest of any mammal migration.

From the lagoons of Baja California where the calves are born, gray whales hug the coastline on their northward journey. The first to pass are adults, reaching up to 49 feet in length. Following behind over the next few months are the cow-calf pairs. By the time the babies reach us, they are about 16 feet in length. The best places for viewing from land are headlands and capes, where elevation gives you a broad vantage. Numerous coastal whale-watch vessels operate from harbors all along the coast.

Gray whales are identified by their mottled, gray appearance and the absence of any prominent dorsal fin. Along the animal's back, look for a ridge of knuckle-like bumps instead. On still days, the blow pattern is a distinctive V-shape, because of twin nostrils on the animal's head. Animals typically surface several times, then take a deeper dive that can last up to five minutes. They travel at about five miles per hour, or about half the speed of a cruising fishing boat.

Gray whales are baleen whales. Instead of teeth, their jaws are lined with plates of fibrous baleen, which act as a sieve to catch food. They feed on the seafloor, rolling sideways to plow up sediments and filtering amphipods and other organisms through the baleen as they expel water and mud from their giant mouths. Some whales remain through summer along the Pacific Northwest Coast, forgoing the long miles northward in favor of good feeding habitat along the way. Gray whale calves are voracious eaters, consuming up to 200–300 gallons of their mothers' rich milk each day. ⭐

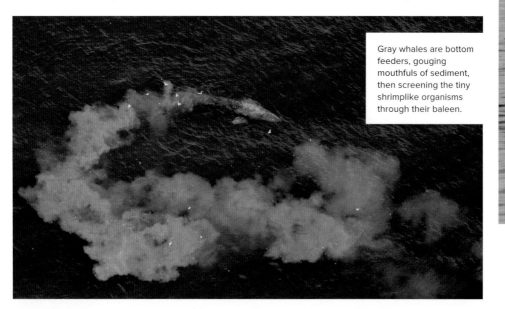

Gray whales are bottom feeders, gouging mouthfuls of sediment, then screening the tiny shrimplike organisms through their baleen.

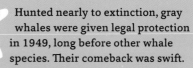

Hunted nearly to extinction, gray whales were given legal protection in 1949, long before other whale species. Their comeback was swift. Although scientists are not sure if current populations match preindustrial whaling abundance, the current number—approximately 23,000 animals—may be at or near the carrying capacity of Northeast Pacific coastal habitat for the whales, given modern ocean conditions.

Buoys, docks, and even boats are common haul-outs.

California sea lion
Zalophus californianus

The California sea lion is one of the most familiar and recognizable of all marine mammals—this is the animal we all first saw as the so-called trained seal, performing tricks and entertaining us on television or at an aquarium with its barks and showman-like antics.

Unlike seals, sea lions have the ability to move on their limbs. The fore- and hind-flippers have articulated joints that rotate to support their weight, allowing them to walk, giving them the mobility that seals lack. California sea lions are also distinguished by small ear flaps and a bulging forehead, larger on males than on females.

Sea lions are very social, gathering in large, often noisy groups. Posing proudly or idly lounging on docks, buoys, or beaches, they are loud and very active, jostling for position in their dense coteries. Males compete for domination over harems of females, showing teeth and growling to intimidate rivals. Older males show scars from previous conflicts, won or lost. Although they can walk on land, they are very clumsy looking. In contrast, underwater, sea lions move with amazing grace, darting and swooping with the agility of a jet fighter.

California sea lions breed in large colonies on offshore rocks and islands along the southern California coast. They migrate to the Pacific Northwest in search of food—often salmon, smelt, or other fish returning to rivers to spawn. We typically see them in spring and summer. Their ability to navigate long coastal journeys is uncanny. Sea lions that had become nuisances by eating too many fish at Seattle's Ballard Locks were captured and returned to California, only to turn around and make the trip back for more Seattle salmon. ★

Changing conditions in the ocean can have a dramatic effect on California sea lions. Warm water currents that affect fish populations can force mothers to feed greater distances from their nurseries, resulting in malnourishment for the pups. In 2015, record numbers of underfed pups were admitted to rehabilitation centers after being left by mothers traveling further in search of prey.

Protected under the Marine Mammal Protection Act in 1972, the California sea lion represents a conservation success story—perhaps too successful. With the population nearing the ocean's carrying capacity, they can pose a threat to endangered salmon runs, resulting in quotas that allow some lethal control where weak salmon stocks are threatened.

common murre

Uria aalge

During summer, offshore rocks and islands all along the coast support large numbers of breeding seabirds, drawn here by the coastal upwelling conditions and fish populations they make possible. The common murre is among the most abundant. Murres are medium in size, with straight, pointed bills. During breeding season, they have black heads, backs, and wings that contrast sharply with their snow-white chests. They spend nearly their entire lives on the water, coming ashore only to lay and incubate their eggs. Mating pairs produce only one offspring per year. Life in the colony is precarious. Adults don't build nests. Instead, the female lays a single egg directly on a cliff ledge or among cliff vegetation. For birds of their size, murres form the densest breeding colonies known. Adults can be packed so tightly on narrow ledges that the animals touch one another. The egg is incubated between the adult's legs as it stands upright, penguin-like. Nature has furnished one adaptation that keeps the eggs from rolling into the sea—they are pointed at one end. When the egg rolls, it simply turns in a circle.

Although common murres are seen throughout the year, breeding flocks leave their colony areas and spread out to sea, where they feed through winter. As spring approaches, they gather on the water near the breeding cliffs, forming into vast flocks. From a distance, listen to their raucous calls. To the naked eye, they resemble ground pepper, floating on the sea surface. Once they take to the nesting grounds, the eggs are incubated for four to five weeks. When the young leave the nest, they don't so much fly off the rocks as tumble. On the water, the juveniles remain with their fathers, learning to fish and fend for themselves. ★

common murre

Common murres are very sensitive to disturbance. Birds flushed off the nesting area by boats or low-flying aircraft can kick eggs off or leave unprotected chicks vulnerable to gulls or eagles. Because they spend so much time on the water, murres are especially vulnerable to oil spills. After the 1991 *Tenyo Maru* oil spill, off Cape Flattery in Washington, estimates on murre fatalities ranged from 4,000 to 17,000 animals. Shifting conditions in the ocean also have an impact on common murre populations by affecting the food sources of forage fish, which the birds depend upon.

Common murres gather on the water near breeding colonies in large flocks.

cormorants

Phalacrocorax species

Cormorants are large diving birds with a peculiar habit of draping their wings as they bask in sunlight. Large breeding colonies occur in many places along the Pacific Northwest Coast. Two species, Brandt's cormorant and the pelagic cormorant are almost exclusively found in coastal habitats. A third, the double-crested cormorant commonly inhabits inland and fresh-water habitats.

Cormorants are shiny black birds that sit upright. They have long necks and sharp, hooked bills, used for snagging fish underwater. As divers, they tuck their wings close to their sides and propel themselves entirely by their webbed feet, in the case of pelagics chasing prey to depths of up to 150 feet. Returning to the surface with a fish, the cormorant will swallow it head first and later regurgitate a pellet of bones and other indigestible material.

Telling the Brandt's and pelagics apart is fairly easy. Brandt's cormorant is larger and has a kink in its neck as if flies. During breeding, Brandt's has a bright blue patch beneath its bill. Pelagics are more diminutive, fly with a straight neck, and, in breeding season, have white patches on their flanks.

Breeding colonies are busy places. Brandt's and pelagics nest high on sea cliffs. Cormorant males gather sticks, but leave the nest construction to the females. The female lays a clutch of eggs, usually three or four. Once the chicks hatch, both parents feed the young. Within the colony, chicks often form their own groups, called crèches. Gradually the crèche gets larger and larger. Scientists suspect that the grouping helps them stay warm and protects the young from predators.

So why do cormorants sun themselves with wings half-spread? Scientists believe that cormorants have less preening oil in their feathers and that the feathers get wet. The behavior could be their way of drying off. ✱

A double-crested cormorant drapes its wings in the sunlight.

glaucous-winged gull
Larus glaucescens

Gull identification is complicated, as there are so many species to choose from. And each species can have different seasonal plumages as well as different color phases for adults and juveniles. On top of that, gulls interbreed with other gull species, blurring the distinction entirely. In other words, gull identification can baffle even experienced birders. The best bet, for beginners, is to pick out one or two common species, get to know them well, and gradually add other gulls once your eye is sharpened to subtle differences in their field marks, seasonality, and behavior. Here's where attention to detail and a good birding field guide are helpful.

The glaucous-winged gull is one of the most common breeding gulls in the Pacific Northwest. It is a large gull and relatively easy to identify by its frost-gray wingtips that match the light gray of its back. Look for pink feet and a stout yellow bill that is slightly thickened at the tip, accented with a red spot.

Glaucous-winged gulls are omnivores, as likely to forage on garbage as they are on small invertebrates or nestlings of other bird species (sometimes even their own). Adults return to their nesting colonies in late spring. In addition to islands and bluffs, glaucous-winged gulls will nest on pilings and roofs in waterfront areas. A pair will nurse a clutch of two or three eggs. The young fledge at about six weeks but remain close to the parents, often begging for food, even once they have reached adult size. Until it reaches breeding age, a juvenile may be difficult to identify as it goes through different plumage phases. ★

glaucous-winged gull

Glaucous-winged gull populations have grown dramatically in the last decades, due to their indifference to people, our built environment, and all of our garbage. Their growing numbers, however, pose a threat to other seabirds with whom they compete for nesting territories and prey on.

Three species of gulls (Heermann's, dark gray; Bonaparte's, small dot on head; and herring, large white) share a rock with black oystercatchers.

harbor seal

Phoca vitulina

Walking along the shore, it occurs to you that you are being watched: a smooth, round head rises out of the water and a seal's soft black eyes fix upon you. Silently, the seal slips under the water, rises a few yards away, and gives you another glance.

Harbor seals evolved from a walking land mammal ancestor sometime around one million years ago. Unlike sea lions, which can move on land with the use of their flippers serving as legs, seals on land must belly-flop from one place to the next. In the water, they are very agile and forage for a wide range of fishes and invertebrates. At haul-out sites on remote or protected beaches, they crowd together, resembling beach logs, grunting and jostling as they bask.

Adults grow to be about 6 feet long and can weigh up to just under 300 pounds. Their fur can range from black to brown to silver, blotched with light or dark spots. Pups are born in spring and can swim almost immediately. Nursed on rich mothers' milk, the pups grow quickly, gradually gaining fishing skills as they explore shallow waters near their home haul-out. ★

Because harbor seals are relatively immobile on land, they are easily disturbed by people and pets. Pups are often left alone by mothers as they seek food. Never assume a baby seal needs to be rescued—that act is most likely a sentence to death or a life in captivity. After the birthing period, seals molt, losing part of their hair and skin and must stay on land during that painful and stressful time. Seals are also susceptible to diseases that can be transmitted to pets or people. Despite their gentle looks, they can be dangerous.

Because harbor seals eat many species of commercially caught fish, they are considered by some to be competitors and are often harassed or even shot, in the mistaken belief that fewer seals means more fish. This view ignores other factors influencing the abundance of fish, including overharvest, habitat loss, and variable ocean conditions. Harbor seals are protected in the United States under the Marine Mammal Protection Act. Harassment is a federal offense.

Harbor seals seek isolated beaches for haul-outs. Unable to walk on land or crawl on rocks, they flop in order to move around.

sea otter

Enhydra lutris

The Pacific Northwest's largest member of the weasel family, sea otters are truly marine mammals and very rarely venture onto land. Instead, they prefer life in the kelp forest, foraging for sea urchins, crabs, shellfish, and other prey. Unlike whales, seals, and sea lions, that have thick blubber for insulation, otters rely on their lush fur to retain body heat. As many as one million hairs per square inch provide warmth and make their fur the densest of any animal. Male otters can reach nearly 5 feet in length and weigh up to 100 pounds. Females are smaller and rarely reach over 75 pounds.

Life in the kelp canopy can appear leisurely, with otters lazing on their backs, often in groups. However, they require as much as a third of their body weight in food each day, enough to keep them busy diving for food and traveling between feeding and resting areas. On the move, they swim much like seals and sea lions, flexing their lower body for propulsion. At rest, they float on their backs, gently paddling with their flipper-like hind paws.

Sea otters depend on kelp forests as their habitat. Thick mats of floating kelp furnish shelter. Otters will often wrap themselves in kelp to keep from drifting off as they sleep. The presence of sea otters is critical to kelp habitat. As the principal predator of sea urchins, they keep the kelp-hungry urchin populations in check and assure the survival of the kelp forest and the ecological integrity of the kelp forest community.

Where sea otters occur—such as Washington's Olympic Coast—look for them in kelp beds. Good places to spot them are at Cape Flattery and, after the four-mile hike, Cape Alava. You'd better use binoculars or a spotting scope however—they like to stay away from shore and have a keen sense of smell that alerts them to danger. An otter on its back looks like a small barge, with head and feet upturned at both ends. Older animals often have whitish fur on their faces. Outside their range, any that you see are almost always river otters, their smaller weasel cousin. River otters almost always swim on their stomachs and, in profile, have pointed faces and long, pointed tails. ★

River otters are common in saltwater environments. Their slimmer form, swimming on their stomach, and more pointed head are easy ways to distinguish them from sea otters, where their ranges overlap.

Once common along the entire Pacific Northwest coastline, sea otters today are limited in range to the northern Olympic Peninsula and the northwestern coast of Vancouver Island. That they occur there is only because they were reintroduced in the 1970s after an absence of over 50 years. Sea otter populations all around the North Pacific Rim were decimated in the nineteenth century by fur hunters. Only small populations in Russia, Alaska, and central California survived. Since they have received legal protection, and with the efforts of conservationists and biologists, otters have been relocated in parts of their former range and thrived.

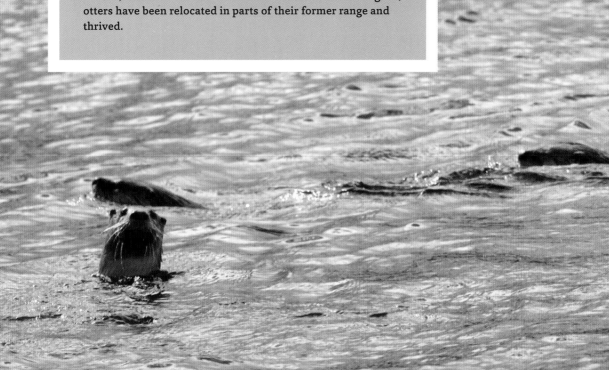

sooty shearwater
Puffinus griseus

Sooty shearwaters are true oceanic birds, migrating from Australia, New Zealand, and Chile to the North Pacific to harvest from our food-rich temperate waters. Their annual migration distance can be as much as 40,000 miles between their nesting grounds and the Pacific Northwest Coast. Most common farther away from shore, they come close enough for us to see from land in a few places like North Head, at the mouth of the Columbia River, and Cape Flattery at Washington's northwest tip.

Smaller than albatrosses, another ocean-roaming migrant, sooty shearwaters share their wing and body characteristics—long, narrow, pointed wings perfect for soaring on the updrafts of air that are strongest just at the crests of waves. Effortlessly, they roller coaster from one wave to the next, dipping into wave troughs sometimes only inches off the water's surface. Because of this low-level gliding ability, they are able to conserve energy by reducing the need to constantly flap their wings to stay aloft.

Sooty shearwaters nest in burrows on islands. After hatching a single baby, both parents feed the youngster until it can fend for itself. Then, the adults abandon the fledgling and begin the migration that takes them quickly through equatorial waters and eventually to the North Pacific continental shelf, just as our seasonal coastal upwelling begins. Here, they feed on small shrimplike crustaceans, squid, and jellyfish. Scientists have tracked these remarkable journeys with radio transmitters, discovering that the migratory pattern isn't simple a straight line to and from. Instead, the annual migration route might be a broad figure-8 that takes in a visit to the Southern Ocean during the austral summer, a stop on the breeding grounds, then a visit to the North Pacific during the northern summer.

Look for these birds from a high cape or headland using your binoculars or spotting scope. Windy conditions bring them closer to shore. At times, vast flocks settle onto the water within view. On the move, they will be flying just at wave-top, the darkened silhouette of long wings and a short body. ★

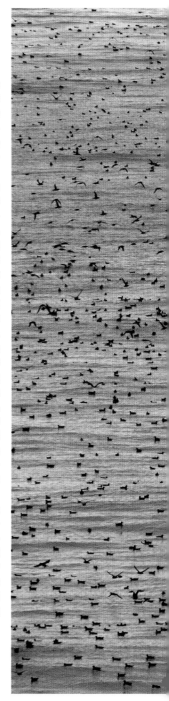

Navigators that arrive from the Southern Hemisphere to feed in productive Northwest waters, sooty shearwaters are sometimes visible in large flocks from headlands like North Head, at the mouth of the Columbia River.

surf scoter
Melanitta perspicillata

No, surf scoters don't surf. At least not the way people surf. But they do spend a lot of time in the surf, foraging for shellfish and riding the froth. Your first reaction to surf scoters will likely be to chuckle. These clown-like black coastal ducks have broad, chunky bills, useful for prying shellfish off rocks when they dive underwater. The male's bill is bright orange at the tip and upper surface, and white along the sides with a black spot. White patches on their head and white eyes complete the picture. The gaudy appearance probably serves to attract a mate. Females are more subdued, with dull black and white markings and without the orange.

Surf scoters are very common and occur in large flocks. We see them

Although surf scoter populations appear to be stable, the sea ducks are vulnerable to oil spills and destruction of their Arctic breeding habitat. Alaska populations declined during the 1990s; chemical contaminants are thought to have been the cause.

often in winter, gathering in large feeding flocks. Scientists have observed that flocks will often dive all at once. This strategy may be a way of outwitting gulls that try to steal their food when they return to the surface—it's harder to thieve from a whole crowd than from a single individual. Their breeding habitat is in Alaska, and the Yukon and Northwest Territories, on freshwater lakes and ponds. During summer, nonbreeding flocks are regular residents near our beaches, jetties, and docks.

Surf Scoter females are known for their casual approach to caring for their young. After breeding, the males leave the nesting grounds. The females brood from four to seven eggs. Once the ducklings hatch, the mothers and hatchlings mingle with other moms and babies—like in a big cooperative preschool. Mix-ups occur among families, but the young are generally cared for by some mother or another. Females then leave the breeding grounds and the young find their way to the coast on their own. ★

Surf scoters feed on mussels and other organisms attached to rocks, exposing them to very rough conditions.

Rivers

Coastal rivers and their watersheds are the liquid circulation system of our region. Ocean-born weather systems replenish the land in the form of rain, snow, and fog. Once delivered, that water is held in reservoirs—glaciers, aquifers, lakes, wetlands, living vegetation, decaying organic matter, and streambeds. Then gravity takes over and the water returns to the ocean, sometimes in a trickle, sometimes in a flood, carving the landscape into familiar furrows of ridges and canyons and sustaining the lush mantle of green—forests, fields, and valleys—that give the Pacific Northwest its evergreen character.

Rivers form complex ecosystems. In their upper reaches, water can reside for periods lasting months as snowpack, and, in the Olympic Mountains, for decades as glaciers. During snowmelt months of late spring and summer, high basins resonate with the sound of water moving over rocks, through high meadows, and into countless tributaries of the river systems. Wet meadows and lakeshores erupt with wildflowers that capture the twin bursts of seasonal moisture and long daylight hours.

These branched rivulets join into mountain streams that flow through the mid-elevation forests, losing elevation quickly. These reaches are cascade-filled canyons where the streams plunge in foamy rapids into crystal-green pools among moss-covered boulders. This ruggedness limits the movement of larger fish, steelhead, bull trout, and coho salmon that migrate to the sea, forming the uppermost spawning habitat for them. It is also the year-round habitat for resident fish—rainbow and cutthroat trout.

Descending into the broad river valleys and their lowland forests, the tributaries continue to converge. Here, their combined force is revealed in sediment—rocks, gravel, and sand—that the water has carved out of the uplands and spread into a broad mantle on the valley floor. Where these valleys break out of the mountains and foothills they begin to meander in broad floodplains. Seasonal freshets, from springtime

The Quinault River forms high in the Olympic Mountains.

mountain snowmelt and intense storm rainfall, bring additional sediment and river channels become dynamic—bending and cutting into new forest territory and abandoning old channels as dry gravel braids.

Reaching the coastal plain and tidewater, they become sluggish. Shiny mudbanks line the shores and the seaward flow of freshwater encounters the up-river tidal flow of saltwater in the daily exchange dictated by the moon and tides.

Finally, the worlds of river and ocean blend. It can be in a deep bay or a shallow sand bar at the end of a sand spit, merging into the breakers. The cycle has completed itself. The ocean has received itself again after the water—its gift to the land—has nourished countless life forms, created scores of distinct living communities and created the many bounties that humans receive from lush forests and fields, rivers teeming with fish, and the water itself—our prime requisite of life.

Nearing the coast, the Hoh River courses along broad gravel bars.

Tide waters rise and fall where fresh and saltwater mix.

After its journey from its distant, arid sources, the Klamath River blends with the Pacific under low maritime fog.

American dipper

Cinclus mexicanus

American dippers are stout gray songbirds that live their entire lives literally within feet of clean, swift-running streams. You will usually see the bird alone, perched on a rock. Watch it lunge into a whirl of foam, popping up moments later to return to its perch with its buggy gleanings in its beak. Underwater, they walk along the bottom of the river or swim, using their wings to propel them. Watch one carefully and you will see it quickly bob up and down—the dipping motion that that gives the bird its name. Some scientists believe their jerky knee bends are a display—when excited, a bird may dip as often as once every second. The behavior appears to be hardwired. Baby birds have been observed dipping even as nestlings. Whatever purpose it serves, they acquire their nervous tic at an early age.

On and in the water they are capable little boaters, making even expert kayakers look awkward. A dipper will tumble into a rapid, ride the current, and dive to pick insect larvae off the rocks. They sometimes wade chest deep in fast-running water and forage for food. Protective membranes over their eyes allow them to see underwater. A gland that excretes oil to the feathers provides waterproofing—you often see a silvery sheen of water pouring over a partly submerged bird.

Dippers nest near swift current. They construct a rough mud hut reinforced and lined with grass, moss, or bark strips on a rock ledge, or, occasionally, a concrete bridge abutment. The female lays a clutch of four to five eggs and incubates them for about two weeks and brings them food in the nest for another three or four weeks. When they outgrow the nest and are ready to try flying, the babies simply tumble into the torrent, bob about until they get oriented, then swim ashore. ★

Dippers' dependence on clean water makes them indicators of water quality. The aquatic insects they prefer thrive only in the cleanest streams. Nowhere are their numbers great; however, in the right habitat, they are easy to spot and impossible to mistake by their twitchy little knee dips.

bald eagle
Haliaeetus leucocephalus

Few birds convey the majesty of the bald eagle in appearance, although to Benjamin Franklin, the eagle—a foraging thief and scavenger of carrion—was not a very majestic symbol of the young nation of his day. Ben's choice would have been the wild turkey, nobler in its wariness, more selective in its choice of food and more honest in obtaining it.

Often, it is the call of the eagle—a whistle-like warble or hawk scream—that first alerts us to their presence on a nearby tree branch. The adult bald eagle is easy to identify by its broad wingspan (up to 6 feet), bold white head, and bright yellow beak. Immature eagles may be as large as adults, but for several years their feathers are dark and mottled.

Bald eagles, in large numbers, are seasonally attracted to Pacific Northwest riverbanks by masses of salmon—salmon running, salmon spawning, and salmon dying on river bars and in backwater eddies. Eagles that breed in Alaska and the Yukon will make a winter trip to the Skagit, or any of dozens of other Northwest rivers in search of salmon because their home rivers freeze. The delivery of ocean minerals and nutrients to the river ecosystem—by way of salmon—often means a stop as eagle muscle, bone, feather, and feces.

And because they are scavengers, and coastal ecosystems are rich with food in the form of waterfowl and decaying marine mammal and fish carcasses, many eagles that breed in the Northwest never leave the region, establishing nesting and feeding territories that sustain them year-round. In rocky coastal habitat, eagles frequently prey on nesting seabirds, competing with gulls for unwary adults or unsupervised chicks. Once the seabird colonies dissipate, they shift their foraging to other food sources.

Resident breeding pairs often return to the same nest—a platform of sticks high in a tree. Some nests are decades old, outliving its original builders and under a constant state of remodel by current occupants. ⭐

Bald eagles were rare and considered at risk of extinction until the late decades of the twentieth century. Malicious killings and pesticides had taken a toll on the birds. Eagle nesting habitat is still heavily protected, but the success story of bald eagles remains a conservation legacy. Ben Franklin's disapproval or not, the majestic bird is now common among us and ever-inspiring in its emblematic power.

beaver

Castor canadenis

Industry. That's how we think of the busy beaver. These furry, flat-tailed architects of dams and lodges alter waterways and create wetlands essential for many other aquatic species, including waterfowl, salmon, and frogs. Even woodpeckers benefit from snags—trees killed by flooding. North America's largest rodent, adult beavers can reach 40 pounds and 3 feet in length. Their rounded bodies and flat tails are key identifying marks. They live in family groups—an adult pair, recent young (kits), and, occasionally, young from several years past. Females give birth to litters of between one and eight kits.

Beavers are most active at night and are shy, so we typically only see the telltale signs of their busy-ness. Besides dams and lodges, be on the lookout for tree stumps, wood chips, beaver "runways" (conspicuous trails in the mud or open channels among wetland vegetation), and scattered sticks, gnawed on both ends and frequently stripped of

The beaver plays an important role in creating and maintaining crucial wetlands—which are some of the most productive terrestrial habitats we know of. Sometimes, that effort is not appreciated—as when trees or shrubs favored by homeowners and foresters are killed, or when beaver dams flood roads and property. Living with beavers isn't that tough, however. Plants can be protected with fencing or wire mesh guards. Landowners can select landscape plants that don't appeal to beavers. In extreme cases where beaver dams flood property, overflow structures can complement the beaver's work by keeping water levels stable, while still meeting the beaver's need for adequate depth. As a last resort, beavers can be successfully relocated by wildlife professionals. Chances are, however, that another busy beaver will move into the territory to take up where the last one left off.

tender bark. In well-established beaver habitat, structures may be hard to spot because willow and other vegetation has taken root in the tangle of sticks placed by the animals.

Look for the animals in the morning or evening. Approach the pond quietly and be on the lookout for movement in the water—often a moving V-shape. Only the nose and eyes will be visible as the animal swims. If you are lucky, the animal may emerge onto land. Although their eyesight is poor, their senses of smell and hearing are sharp. ★

Side channels and beaver ponds create important habitat within coastal river valleys. Protected from winter floods in the rivers themselves, these are refuges for young fish and support many other aquatic and forest animals.

caddis fly
Trichoptera

Study a shallow cobble-lined stream channel carefully. Look for small insect larval cases made of fine bits of grit or organic material sticking to the rocks (often called periwinkles). Pick one up and look at it under a magnifying glass. It's a tube, made of fine particles. Sticking out of its fat end, notice the head and forelegs of the caddis larva safe within its casing. What you are looking at is an insect. What you are seeing is a sign of clean water and an indicator of a healthy aquatic insect population and food chain.

Caddis flies are a large group of aquatic insects (12,000 species worldwide) that spend most of their lives in the water, emerging as mothlike flying insects. Life for a caddis fly has four stages: egg, larva, pupa, and adult. Of all their life stages, only the larvae eat, capturing tiny food particles suspended in the water. To make their cases, caddis fly larva produce saliva that binds to small grains of sand or organic material. The tubular case grows as they grow. After the larvae mature, they close their cases with silk and become inactive for weeks or months. Triggered by a change in water temperature, the pupas emerge, cutting open their cases with specialized jaws and swimming or floating to the surface. A caddis fly "emergence" occurs when masses of pupae leave their cases at the same time. Hungry fish prey on the vulnerable insects during this phase, gobbling them up as they shed their pupal case and unfurl their wings.

For those that make it to the surface as adults, life is short—only one or two weeks—just enough time to mate. In that time, the insects mate and the female lays a mass of eggs. As adults they are most active at night, and fly in erratic flight paths—tempting morsels for hungry fish. ★

Adult caddis flies resemble moths more than flies. Emerging in large numbers when conditions are right, they provide a burst of nutrients to fish and, if not eaten, reproduce and die within a few short weeks.

Rivers

coho salmon

Oncorhynchus kisutch

Seven species of the salmon genus *Oncorhynchus* ("on-co-rink-us," meaning "hooked nose") inhabit Pacific Northwest coastal waters and rivers. Salmon spawn in freshwater, migrate to the ocean, and return to their birth waters to lay eggs and die. Of the salmon, coho exemplify this river-to-ocean-and-back-again life history. Here, they spend about as much time in the river system as juveniles as they spend in ocean, growing to their full adult size. A typical life cycle for a coho in the Pacific Northwest includes several months incubating as an egg, just over a year in the river system as fry and fingerlings (juveniles), and about the same time in the ocean.

Coho movements are usually in response to flow rates. High rainy season flows push the young fish into quieter side channels, tributaries, and beaver ponds—or downstream. After leaving the river system, their saltwater movements begin close to shore near their home river and gradually lengthen. After a full year at sea growing to adult size, they return to their

Between the time it emerged from the river gravel as a fry and the time it dried on the river bank, this salmon traveled hundreds of miles in the ocean and returned to spawn. In addition to another generation of salmon, its gifts to the river and forest were precious nutrients.

birth river when higher flows draw them upstream to the spawning grounds.

Although highly adapted to their specific river environments, coho display many characteristics of a more primitive freshwater salmonid ancestor. Coho are aggressive predators, even as fry, eating a variety of insects and smaller fish, including other salmon fry. During their time in freshwater, they occupy territories that they defend against smaller fish or surrender to larger fish. While rainy season floods swell the main channels of their home river, they find their way into quieter backwaters of food-rich small streams, side channels, and ponds.

Returning coho present a spectacle as they move upstream. They enter the river and move as a large group, pressing higher and higher into the river system. They wriggle over shallow riffles and leap high over cascades. Finally, where the gravel and water flow are just right, they spawn the next generation and die.

That death is not the end, however. Coho salmon, fattened on zooplankton and small fish in the ocean, return those nutrients to the forest once the streamside scavengers—eagles, ravens, bears, and a host of other animals—recycle them back into the river and forest landscape. ★

Over the course of a century, the conservation of coho populations has shifted from a strong emphasis on hatchery production to habitat protection and strengthening—not replacing—wild fish stocks. Coho's dependence on small tributaries, side channels and beaver ponds during their freshwater life phase as fry means that larger areas of river corridor need protection. And run timing (the adaptation of generations returning to the same river at the optimal time for spawning) gives wild coho an evolutionary advantage for survival.

common merganser

Mergus merganser

I was once drifting on an easy current in a whitewater raft when a swift flight of common mergansers rounded the bend downstream and flew just off the water toward the raft with powerful beating wings. Just when I thought I'd be impaled by one of the fish-duck's razor bills, the panicked squadron split apart, passing us on two sides. Who was more startled, us or them?

Common mergansers are fish-eating ducks of the rivers. Like my encounter, they are often seen flying at riffle-top and great speed along the river corridor. Both sexes have slim bodies and trim wings. Their duckbills are long and pointed with a slight hook at the end and serrations along the edges of upper and lower jaws. Breeding males are bright white, with black on the back, a dark green head, and a brilliant orange bill. Females have gray bodies and red-brown heads with a fuzzy crest the back. Look for a white chin patch and slender orange bill.

Common mergansers are abundant on our coastal rivers, but rare in saltwater, although they will sometimes winter in coastal estuaries. They are forest-cavity nesters, using hollowed trees or holes made and abandoned by pileated woodpeckers. Egg clutches vary from six to over a dozen eggs. Chicks abandon the nest within days of hatching, tumbling to the forest floor, and, guided by the mother, find their way to water. During breeding season it is common to see a female leading a procession of ducklings along the eddy lines of the river current. For their first few weeks, the ducklings feed on insects, snails, and other small invertebrates before they shift to small fish, including salmon fry, which form their principal diet as adults.

Common mergansers are just one species that depends on tree cavities for nesting. Mature forests that line our coastal rivers have trees of varying ages and stages of life, death and decay. Over 80 species of North American birds require tree cavities for nesting. These include ducks, owls, woodpeckers, raptors, swifts, chickadees, nuthatches, wrens, and warblers. Many of these birds are year-round residents and essential players in the ecological communities of forest, river, and shore. Riparian buffer zones—swaths of undisturbed forest that line our rivers—are critical to "populations" of cavity-bearing trees and the populations of avian wildlife they sustain.

osprey
Pandion haliaetus

At first, the silhouette soaring over the river looks like a small eagle. But the kink in its wings immediately tells us that this fish hunter is an osprey—eagle of eye and sharp of talon—and equally lethal to unwary fish.

Besides size and wing shape, other markings that make the osprey easy to identify are its mix of dark and light feather patterns beneath the wing and a pronounced dark eye strip across its white head. The sharp, hooked beak is black. Not easily visible, osprey feet have one toe that reverses, enabling it to grip its prey more firmly in its talon hooks.

Osprey hunt very methodically, using their keen eyesight to find fish in the water from aloft. A solitary bird will patrol in circles or on long zigzags over open water. Often, after sighting its prey, it will pause momentarily to hover, before folding its wings in a controlled fall, talons first. Grasping the fish, the bird may be entirely submerged before it struggles back into the air and takes wing to fly to its perch or nest with a writhing fish in its claws. A caught fish usually gets an aerial view during its last minutes—the osprey grips the fish so the fish flies headfirst, reducing the air drag.

Osprey nests are broad platforms made of sticks easily confused with the nest of the bald eagle. Old nests may, in fact, have been used alternately by both species over the generations. Although they prefer fish, look beneath osprey nests for clam shells, crab parts, or other castoff remains of amphibians and other nonfish food items. ★

red alder

Alnus rubra

Red alder is the pioneer tree of the riverbank. Throughout the coastal Pacific Northwest, where river floods braid through the broad valley bottoms, you will find this common tree. On the raw sand and gravel of a freshly scoured riverbank, alder sprouts into dense thickets of saplings whose roots bind the loose river-laid sediment. Left undisturbed, the trees eventually thin out and mature into tall stands of gray-white tree trunks supporting a leafy canopy.

Alder plays another important role as a pioneer by adding nutrients to barren, disturbed soils. It does this in two steps. The first step is with the help of bacteria that infect alder roots and produce tiny coral-like clusters of nodules in the root system. In the nodules, atmospheric nitrogen is converted into ammonia by the bacteria. The nutrients help the alder grow. The second step involves the organic material, in the form of leaves, limbs, and decomposing wood that alder trees contribute to the forest soil. Although alders may only live 40–50 years, in that time they transform sand and gravel into forest soils that support a host of grasses, ferns, shrubs, and young conifers.

Alder "bottoms," spacious stands on river-valley floors, form important habitat for a host of forest animals, including amphibians, small mammals, and songbirds. Understory plants, including grasses and shrubs, like salmonberry and elderberry, are heavily foraged by elk and deer. Early spring growth of many of these plants is due to a time lag between the time they issue new growth and the time that the alder canopy fully leafs out, shading the forest floor. Elk particularly favor lush alder forest habitat in the early spring.

Though not as dense as maple, alder wood is a commonly used hardwood because of its clear white color and workability. And the rich flavor imparted by thick alder smoke gives Pacific Northwest seafood, from fire-roasted salmon to smoked oysters, their particular regional flavors. ★

River valley alder groves are open to sunlight during winter months when they are without leaves. Before the springtime "green up," light enters the forest floor coaxing a burst of growth among understory plants.

river otter
Lutra canadensis

Three small heads and one large one are cutting Vs across the current in a slow-moving river. It's a litter of young river otter pups, being herded by a wary parent. The small one at the rear yips as it tries to catch up to the others. The adult circles back to collect it.

Known for their sleekness and agility, river otters are common in most aquatic environments in the Pacific Northwest, including saltwater. They are well adapted for swimming, paddling with their webbed feet, and snaking their long, slender bodies and tapered tails to move with ease in the water. On land, they walk or bound, arching their backs in a loping gait.

River otters have voracious appetites, eating a wide variety of fish, including salmon and trout. They also prey on frogs, aquatic invertebrates, and, occasionally, bird eggs, babies, or molting adult ducks. Food moves through them quickly—a trip through their stomach and intestines can take as little as an hour.

In areas frequented by river otters, look for communal heaps of feces containing well-chewed bits of fish bones and scales and other slimy food remnants. Such piles smell strongly of—you guessed it—fish. Other otter signs to look for are five-toed tracks, trails through mud and underbrush, and slides on mud banks. River otters den in logjams, among boulders or logs partially covered by mudslides, and abandoned lodge or dens of beaver and other animals. Although generally shy around humans, they also frequent docks and moored boats and will den in accessible spaces under buildings and porches.

Even though they are common in saltwater where their range overlaps with sea otters, river otters are easily distinguished from their larger marine relatives. River otters have long, pointed tails that often whip in the air as they dive; sea otters have a blunt, rudder-like tail. River otters' heads are smaller, with pointed snouts; sea otters have squarish heads, with blonde or white fur in the face. Sea otters most often swim on their backs, although they will sometimes porpoise (leap and plunge) when swimming quickly over distances; River otters rarely swim on their backs, although they may roll or somersault when diving or chasing prey. Sea otters very rarely leave the water; river otters may roam as far as a half mile inland from shore. ★

River otters are also common in saltwater, where they move from water to land—and docks—with ease.

Estuaries

Estuaries of the Pacific Northwest vary greatly in scale, from the combined inland seas of Georgia Strait and Puget Sound—the Salish Sea—to the tiny mouth of a coastal stream that swells with the incoming tide and empties to a mud-lined trickle at ebb.

The common characteristic of all estuaries is that they are mixing zones where freshwater coming off the land blends with the ocean's saltwater. The ever-changing salinity, driven by cycles of river runoff and flood in the watershed systems and surge and inundation by sea and tide, make the estuary, as an ecosystem, one of the ultimate "edge" environments—here, the aquatic systems of land and sea overlap.

Living organisms whose bodies must tolerate change in salt levels face one of the most demanding challenges of all, because salt affects how organisms function at a cellular level. Salt draws water out of our cells, the way a hot sun dries a leaf. Plants, invertebrates, fishes, and birds—any organism exposed to variations in the salt they ingest or that surrounds them must withstand great stress to their very cells, tissues, and organs.

And yet, estuaries form some of the richest habitat in terms of biodiversity and abundance of living things. Rivers carry more than water; they transport sediments and nutrients. Where the water reaches sea level, it slows, dropping its sediment load. This creates the mudflats we see at low tide in estuaries. It also creates turbidity—cloudiness in the water from suspended particles. Those sediments, locked in the mud or suspended in the water, are rich with nutrients found in organic material and minerals.

Marine life that thrives in the estuary environment uses these nutrients in a variety of ways. In the uppermost sunlit layers of water, phytoplankton grows, forming a complex food chain that sustains drifting zooplankton and progressively larger organisms including fishes and fish predators, as large as orca whales. On the estuary floor, filter feeders, like clams and oysters, pump water through their siphons and glean suspended nutrients. They are consumed by fish and crabs. Within the estuary seabed mud itself, burrowing organisms like worms tunnel into and pass sediment through their gut, extracting nutrients and excreting fine particles of indigestible organic and inorganic material. Burrowing organisms are consumed by gray whales and, where they can be extracted, by shorebirds.

Each of these nutrient pathways within the estuary creates feeding opportunities for whole chains of animals, from minute carnivorous fish and shellfish larvae all the way to smaller predators like shorebirds and

Estuary mudflats are major fueling stations for shorebirds that weigh mere ounces yet must migrate thousands of miles.

Estuaries

larger ones like seals, sea lions, whales, and even humans, the greatest beneficiaries of food energy produced in the marine environment.

This frenzy of feeding is regulated by many cycles. On a daily basis, tidal cycles expose and conceal estuary mudflats. At low tide, shorebirds have access to estuary food sources. At high tide, fish patrol the same beds. High tides that flood the estuary with saltwater push juvenile salmon, not yet fully adapted to saltwater, toward fresher headwaters. At low tide, when freshwater input is greater, they feed in the deeper channels where freshwater flows.

Estuary cycles are also regulated by the journeys that many animals take in their migratory cycles dictated by their life histories. Shorebirds and waterfowl spend winters in mild southern climates migrating north to capture the nutrient energy pulse of the short Arctic summer—the food necessary to breed offspring and nourish them through their juvenile stages. For them, estuaries are the fueling stations that provide the energy needed for their annual journeys.

Rich sediments settle in estuaries, producing boot-sucking mud—and homes for burrowing organisms.

Pacific Northwest salmon life histories are divided into phases of riverine and ocean existence. They hatch and hide as fry as freshwater fish; they mature and fatten in ocean pastures as saltwater fish. Then they spawn and die, once-again freshwater fish. Their journeys, which take them far into the ocean, are marked with estuary stages. Chinook salmon enter estuaries early in their life, as tiny fry, gradually adapting to the saltwater environment. In estuaries, they grow in size and strength, both necessary for ocean survival. Returning from the sea, salmon pass through the estuaries of their home rivers, lingering until river flows signal that conditions are right for upriver travel and spawning.

As rich and necessary as estuaries are for their living dependents, they also pose hazards as a result of human activity. They are the collection basins of whole watersheds, receiving polluted runoff containing excess nutrients from fertilizer used on farms and lawns. They receive high loads of toxics, the daily-used chemicals of urbanized, industrialized societies and their sprawling impermeable landscapes of pavement and rooftops. Just as estuaries concentrate beneficial nutrients, they concentrate pollutants, sequestering them in sediments and suspending them in the water column. Poor estuary water quality is tragically evident in bioaccumulated toxins present in top predators: the living tissues of orca whales contain enough chemical toxins to make whale flesh itself a toxic substance. Estuary health is a huge societal challenge. Cleanups of urbanized Georgia Strait, Puget Sound, Grays Harbor, and the Columbia River estuaries are permanent processes as we try to repair past and prevent present forms of human insult. Even smaller estuaries, like Willapa Bay, Tillamook Bay, Coos Bay, and others of the rural, timbered coastal regions suffer from nutrient overload and siltation attributable to agriculture and forest practices.

As we consider estuaries, however, a bright spot remains. For nearly a century, throughout the Pacific Northwest, estuary mudflats were considered wastelands, to be diked or filled and converted into dry land—farms, industrial areas, cities, and neighborhoods. During that time, estuaries were dumping grounds for waste liquors from pulp mills, sawdust from sawmills, and garbage and sewage from towns and burgeoning cities of the region. We have at least halted most of that by recognizing the ecological and economic benefits of tidelands, salt marshes, and healthy waters where rivers and ocean mix. The bounties of salmon and shellfish the Northwest is known for require healthy estuaries; the scenic and recreational amenities we expect as a Pacific Northwest birthright depend on estuaries. Most of all, the host of living organisms, from lugworms, deep in the mudflat mire, to orca whales, breaching into sight, rely on estuaries for their existence.

black brant

Branta bernicla

The black brant is a small, dusky-black sea goose that depends on Pacific Northwest estuaries for its favored food, eelgrass. Brant visit us during winter months, as well as fall and spring migration seasons, gathering in flocks on the estuary edge. They breed in the Arctic. The Latin name, given by the great naturalist Linnaeus, combines an old Anglo-Saxon word *brenan*, meaning "charred or burnt" (for the color), and gives a nod to folklore surrounding the goose's origins— hatched from a barnacle. Linnaeus certainly knew better—birds aren't barnacles and barnacles aren't birds.

The stocky little goose is recognizable by its black head and conspicuous white ring around its neck. The breast is white with the wings and back shading to dark gray. Oddly, evolution has equipped them—like sharks, marine reptiles, and other seabirds—with a salt gland that lets them drink saltwater. The specific mechanisms are different in each animal group, but each illustrates the ability of living, evolving organisms—over time—to adapt to specific conditions in their habitats.

Brant are very social, dabbling in the nearshore or wading the shallows, conversing among themselves with soft croaks and crucks. Flying, they lack the discipline of other geese, stringing along loosely or in bunches without forming the V-formation characteristic of other far-ranging waterfowl. ★

Brant have very specific habitat requirements in their winter and breeding ranges. The dredging and filling of coastal wetlands in California, Oregon, and Washington significantly reduced estuary—and eelgrass— habitat available to them. The loss of this wintering habitat has historically taken its toll. In the Arctic, coastal wetlands and tundra are threatened by oil and gas development. Throughout their migratory range, oil spills could have a devastating effect on the entire migrating populations, which numbers somewhere around 125,000 birds.

Chinook salmon

Oncorhynchus tshawytscha

Chinook salmon

Known as "tyee," "blackmouth," or simply as "king," the Chinook is regal among salmon. It is the largest (historically up to 100 pounds), longest lived (up to seven years), and farthest traveled; it spawns in the fastest currents, in the largest gravel, and, tragically, as a species, is the most threatened, often because of stream and estuary habitat loss.

Although Chinook salmon are best known to us during their adult lives as river dwellers—the biggest salmon in the biggest rivers—they are important estuary dwellers in their juvenile and prespawning adult life stages.

The Chinook's overall life history is similar to coho and other salmon species. It emerges out of eggs in freshwater rivers as a fry and, when it enters the estuary, goes through physiological changes that allow it to survive in salt water (the process of becoming a "smolt"). Eventually it migrates to the ocean to grow into an adult, and finally, returns to its birth-stream to spawn and die. Unlike the others, many Chinook (so-called ocean-type Chinook) extend their time in estuaries, both as juveniles and as returning adults. A Chinook's ocean journey may last as much

as four years. The benefit of all that time in the marine environment is massive size, and the strength to migrate up the strongest and longest rivers.

Estuary life for Chinook can begin shortly after emerging as fry from the spawning gravel. Swept into the saltwater environment, they adapt to the saltwater quickly, growing more rapidly than those that remain in the stream. The rich fauna of small insects and marine invertebrates fattens them quickly and the cover of eelgrass beds and tidal salt marshes provide cover for the vulnerable fry. They may spend as much as 18 months in the estuary, moving into shallows at high tide and retreating into deeper channels at low tide. This prolonged estuary residence is of great advantage in their long ocean journeys.

Some Chinook forego the long ocean journey, remaining within neighboring coastal waters or large estuaries, like Puget Sound, returning to home rivers before fully maturing. Named blackmouths, because of their distinctive black gums, these immature Chinook use the estuary environment as if it were the ocean. ⭐

Protecting estuaries is critical to maintaining and restoring Chinook populations. Estuary restoration efforts that include removing dikes and flooding former salt marshes has reopened much juvenile Chinook habitat. For blackmouths, however, even adequate physical habitat may not be enough—pollutants that accumulate within large estuary systems continue to pose a threat.

This young Chinook will spend a significant part of its life growing in estuary waters. Following its life at sea, the estuary will be the next-to-last stage of life before it returns to its native river.

Dungeness crab
Metacarcinus magister

Succulent to eat, but feisty to encounter, Dungeness crab is synonymous with the Pacific Northwest. Ranging from Alaska to Point Conception, California, the largest crabs grow near the center of the range in Washington and Oregon. Although much of the commercial crab harvest occurs in coastal waters, Dungeness crabs are very common in estuaries. Patrolling along on sandy bottoms, they feed on clams and scavenge other food located with the aid of their acute sense of smell.

Dungeness crabs are armored with a tough shell, or carapace, which they outgrow periodically as they mature in a process called molting. Shedding the carapace, legs, and all, the shell splits and the soft-bodied crab eases out backward, leaving its gills in the old shell. Until the new shell forms, the crab is very vulnerable, so it buries itself in the sand until its new carapace has hardened. Mass molting occurs seasonally. Females are timed to molt in spring, males in late summer. Under some conditions, abandoned shells wash up in large quantities, leading beachcombers to assume that there has been a massive die-off of crabs. Close examination reveals that the wash-ups are simply the cast-off shells of molting crabs.

Crabs are very aggressive and won't hesitate to advance, pinchers at the ready, toward what they perceive as a threat. Handling them requires quickness. Experts flip them on their back and grasp the rear of the animal. Even then, a well-placed pinch will teach you a lesson—crabs really are crabby. ★

Feel free to enjoy your crab salad without worrying about the strength of crab populations. Dungeness crabs are rated as "sustainable" by the Monterey Bay Aquarium Seafood Watch Program. Crabbing is very popular and requires a license. Seasons, limits, and size and sex restrictions ensure that populations remain at a sustainable level. Make sure you consult local regulations before you harvest.

eelgrass
Zostera marina

At high tide, the estuary resembles just another wave-covered body of water. But beneath that wavy surface, meadows of grass flutter gracefully, and, like meadows on land, form rich habitat for many fishes, invertebrates, and waterfowl. The grass is eelgrass. It grows at lower tidal levels, shallows that receive abundant sunlight. Unlike most seaweeds, eelgrass is a true flowering plant, forming blossoms and seeds that are dispersed by the current.

Eelgrass blades grow from a tangled system of runners and roots binding the loose sand and silt of the estuary seabed. Thin blades grow to about 3 feet in length and are rounded at the tip. Eelgrass blossoms form along within a sheath. As the seeds mature they split open the sheath and drift away, falling to the bottom. If not eaten, the seeds germinate quickly, sending a shoot upward and tiny root hairs into the sediment.

Eelgrass meadows provide structure—an essential part of all habitat. One-celled algae attach to the ribbon-like blades and form a scummy coating that attracts snails, nudibranchs, and other grazers. The dense foliage provides refuge for crabs, shrimp, and small fish as diverse as flounder, bay pipefish, and juvenile Chinook salmon that avoid larger predators by darting among the mazes of foliage. Eelgrass forms the diet for black brant, a goose entirely dependent on eelgrass habitat and whose populations have dwindled in direct proportion to eelgrass habitat loss. ★

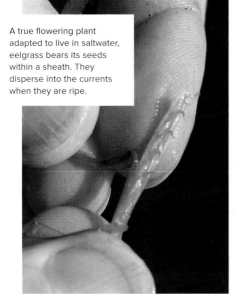

A true flowering plant adapted to live in saltwater, eelgrass bears its seeds within a sheath. They disperse into the currents when they are ripe.

Eelgrass shelters many organisms, including the bay pipefish, a relative of sea horses, that has adapted to blend in to the swaying blades.

eelgrass

Historically, eelgrass has been harvested and used as forage for cattle, thatch for roofs, soundproofing for New York City's Radio City Music Hall, and even as stuffing for early Volkswagen seats. However, water pollution, the dredging and filling of wetlands, shore hardening, and shellfish dredging have taken the greatest toll on eelgrass habitat. Even though vast areas of eelgrass habitat have been lost, protected estuary areas and active restoration of beds have slowed the rate of eelgrass habitat loss and repaired some of the habitat destruction.

great blue heron
Ardea herodias

great blue heron

Few Pacific Northwest birds are easier to recognize than the great blue heron. Stalking prey in shallow water it has the poise of a ballet dancer. Flying, neck tucked awkwardly in an S and sounding loud croaks, it has the grace of a transport plane. The great blue heron is common near rivers, marshes, coastlines, and estuaries. This cosmopolitan resident is found wherever water is nearby.

Great blue herons are our largest herons, bigger than their shy relative, the black-crowned night heron, many times over. Mature birds reach 4 feet in height, with a wingspan of 6 feet. Their feathers are richly layered shades of pale- to dark bluish-gray with a spray of white plumes on the head. Their dagger beak is bright yellow.

Hunting, herons are a study in patience and concentration. They wade with deliberate steps, placing one foot, pausing, then placing the next. Motionless, its retracted neck is in a recoiled position, the bird is perfectly still. Only the eyes move, the bird's keen binocular vision detecting the slightest movements. Then, with stunning quickness, the beak arrows toward its prey, a small fish or crustacean. Spearing or grasping the morsel in its beak, it juggles, then swallows its fresh meal and moves on.

Great blue herons are often solitary or in pairs. When it's nesting time, however, it's another story. Herons are colony nesters, with as many as a hundred birds sharing one or several adjacent nesting trees. The loosely built stick nest is a joint effort between the male and female. He gathers the sticks, and lining material of twigs and foliage; she arranges the nest. Colony trees are used year after year and are raucous places, with the noise of herons coming and going and perching among limbs high in the trees. ★

Heron plumage was popular as a decoration for women's hats at the turn of the twentieth century, which encouraged wide-scale slaughter of herons and other plumed birds by commercial hunters. Responding, forward-thinking conservationists in both the United States and Canada recognized the threat to herons and other birds as early as 1916, when a treaty, the Migratory Birds Convention, was signed by both nations. The treaty has been updated several times and, in addition to international and federal protection in both countries, provinces and states have strengthened laws to protect migrating and nonmigrating birds.

Lewis's moon snail
Euspira lewisii

The moon snail is the largest snail we will encounter in the Pacific Northwest—on land or in the marine environment. These baseball-sized spheres live in sand- and silt-bottomed habitats common in estuaries. Here, they prey on a variety of food sources, but show preference for clams and other shellfish.

Moon snails prowl the seafloor, looking for signs of prey buried in the sediment. Upon detection, they dig rapidly with their massive muscular foot that can expand to nearly four times the volume of their shell. Grasping the prey, a clam for example, they pull it to the surface and suffocate it. Using a specialized boring organ that grows on a stalk on its proboscis, the snail drills a small countersunk hole through the shell and into the clam's meaty body. Scientists believe that chemical enzymes assist the boring process by softening the shell material. The borehole is just large enough to allow the proboscis to enter the shell, and scrape and eat the clam, inside out.

Moon snails prey on a wide variety of shellfish, including small snails and large clams. They display great finesse in locating the precise place to drill— look on discarded clamshells for a neat hole, next to the hinge.

Moon snails are obvious when you find them: a large spiraled shell, surrounded by the massive, jellylike, mucous-covered foot. Often, it is the egg case or "collar" that we find. Marvels of construction, moon snail egg collars require many hours to form. Below the surface of the sand, the female lays a mass of eggs, which she shapes into a mat encircling the outside of her shell. Mucous binds the eggs with sand. Once the collar surrounds her, she pushes it to the surface and applies more mucous to the outside of the ring, securing the eggs in a matrix of sand and abandoning the collar. Over the course of a week, the eggs hatch and the tiny larvae grow. Gradually, the collar disintegrates, releasing the babies as plankton, to drift in the water for about a month. Once their adult features begin to form, the settle to the seafloor and, as tiny snails, begin hunting, and boring into, their prey. ★

Moon snails go to great trouble to shape their egg cases, binding sand with mucous to protect the eggs. Gradually, the collar disintegrates, releasing the eggs to the current.

Estuaries

littleneck clam

Protothaca staminea

Two species of littleneck clam are common in cobble beach areas of our coast and large estuaries—native and Manila littlenecks. Both are popularly known to cooks and connoisseurs as "steamers," clams best steamed lightly in the shell. Of the two, the native is larger and, some say, sweeter. Both species can be distinguished from other hard-shell clams by patterns on the surface of the shell. Littlenecks have fine ridges that radiate out from the hinge area crossed by low ridges that run concentrically. The lookalike heart cockle has only radiating ribs; butter clams have only concentric ridges.

Littleneck clams are filter feeders, drawing water through a siphon—a tube that protrudes out of the shell. They pass slightly more than a quart of water per hour when submerged. They live on minute phytoplankton suspended in the water.

Manila littlenecks were introduced in the 1930s and thrive now on all of our coastal shores. They are the most common steamer in stores and restaurants. They tolerate a wider range of water-chemistry conditions and, according to some, live higher on the beach. ★

Littleneck lookalikes. Smaller, sometimes darker Manila clams were introduced from Asia and now dominate the steamer clam market in the Pacific Northwest.

Recreational shellfish harvests are carefully regulated to prevent overharvest. Licenses are required and minimum sizes are enforced to make sure that only mature clams (having spawned at least once) are taken. Because they are filter feeders, they are accurate monitors of water quality. Clams can consume—and store in their tissue—toxic plankton (commonly known as "red tide") as well as pathogens like *E. coli*, a bacteria that comes from untreated human sewage and animal feces. Clam harvest areas are regularly monitored by health departments to assure that shellfish can be safely consumed. A shellfish closure usually means that the water is polluted.

lugworm

Abarenicola pacifica

The lugworm is just one of many worms and invertebrates that make mudflats so bountiful. And while a bare mudflat may appear to lack eelgrass and other structure that we associate with rich habitat, the mud itself forms the structure needed for a wide variety of burrowing organisms—and the predators they attract.

The lugworm is a segmented worm between 2 and 4 inches in length. The animal is tapered at both ends and varies from pink to yellow-orange to green and brown in color. The worms have a bristled appearance due to paired gills along each side of the body.

Lugworms inhabit the middle and lower intertidal zones of the estuary mudflat, burrowing into the soft sediments. Lugworms are ecosystem engineers. Their borehole forms a U-shaped shaft with openings on both ends. Within the burrow, they ingest mud and silt, rich with organic material. Their digestive system gleans nutrients and they push fecal castings rich in bacteria and undigested organic material to the surface. The castings look like wiggly, thin strings of squeezed toothpaste. A square yard of mud may contain as many as 200 individuals, whose collective efforts till large amounts of sediment, allowing oxygen into otherwise sealed mud. Lugworms in one study were able to completely rework estuary mud to a depth of about 4 inches in 100 days.

Lugworms are among the preferred prey for long-billed shorebirds that migrate through Pacific Northwest estuaries. Probing for burrows as they wade, these hunters are rewarded with fat, succulent lugworms, each yielding a small amount of food—critical fuel for the birds' long migrations. ✦

Exposed mudflats of estuaries appear to be barren wastelands—enough so that, historically, large areas in our coastal estuaries were filled in order to be put to "more productive" uses: agriculture, industry, and tracts of homes. Here, "productivity" was sadly misunderstood. Estuary mudflats are some of the most productive habitats we know of, in terms of the diversity and biomass they support.

Mudflat foragers, like the lesser yellowlegs, probe the mud in search of lugworms and other burrowers.

orca

Orcinus orca

Observing orca whales is a true spectacle of the wild ocean. Often, when we encounter them, they are traveling in groups, rising and diving in rhythm, shimmering black and white as water pours off their smooth bodies. Other common behaviors include spyhopping, tail-lobbing, and breaching. Orcas are toothed whales—actually, the largest species of dolphin. Their distinctive black outline and white markings, erect dorsal fins, and social nature make them hard to confuse with other whales.

The Pacific Northwest is home to two very different populations: the southern residents and the transients. Each group travels over wide areas, both along the Pacific Coast and inside the inner waters of the region. Southern residents typically spend more time in the inland waters of Puget Sound, Georgia Strait, and the Strait of Juan de Fuca—the Salish Sea. Comprised of three major pods, the residents are hunters of fish, particularly the strong salmon runs that return to Fraser River and other Georgia Strait and Puget Sound rivers. The transient orcas roam more offshore, but also frequent the inland waters, preying on marine mammals—seals, sea lions, and other whales.

Social bonds among orcas are very strong. Young whales remain in the company of mothers, grandmothers, aunts, and uncles for much of their lives. As pack hunters, they communicate to coordinate their movements and hunting. Researchers have noted that the residents and transients even communicate in different "dialects" of clicks and squeals, suggesting that differences between the groups have formed over a long period of time, and may indicate greater genetic differences among them.

Many whale-watch operators work out of the region's ports and harbors. Boats from Canada and the United States cooperate in locating the animals. Cruises in the San Juans and Gulf Islands from Victoria, Friday Harbor, and Anacortes offer good chances to observe and learn about these remarkable animals. ★

The constant pressure of vessel traffic on orca pods can cause stress and interfere with communications among pods. Researchers study orcas to understand human impacts and the general health of the populations.

Although long-lived as individuals, orca populations have steadily dwindled in the inner Pacific Northwest waters. Sound pollution, chemical pollution, and the variable salmon population are all thought to stress the populations. Orca pods can be observed from land in many places, particularly the San Juan and Gulf Islands and narrow passages in Puget Sound. Orcas are protected in both the United States and Canada, with strict rules about allowable approach distances and harassment.

Pacific oyster

Crassostrea gigas

The shellfish of Pacific Northwest estuaries have sustained humans for thousands of years. In the 1850s, miners of the California Gold Rush ate Pacific Northwest oysters after beds in San Francisco Bay were depleted by overharvest. Today, the estuaries of Barkley Sound, Puget Sound, Willapa Bay, Netarts Bay, and Yaquina Bay produce abundant commercial crops of oysters, renowned the world over for their distinctive succulence. Oysters form the most important shellfish crop in our economy.

The Pacific oyster is native to Japan, and not the Pacific Northwest. It was introduced to the region in the 1920s after the collapse of the Olympia oyster due to overharvest, disease, and water pollution. Although the smaller Olympias are making a comeback thanks to habitat restoration and market demand, Pacifics, which are more tolerant of environmental conditions, easier to grow, and larger, have become the principal oyster of our region both for commercial growing and recreational harvesting, where that is permitted.

Oysters are filter feeders, drawing water through their digestive system and screening out nutrients. Filtered water passes back out. An adult oyster is capable of filtering nearly one and a half gallons of water per hour. The upside is that oysters actively clean water; a downside is that when toxic algae or bacteria are in the water, oysters themselves become contaminated—and unfit for human consumption. Water quality is closely monitored and harvest times regulated for both recreational and commercial gatherers to assure that human health is not compromised. ★

Estuaries

231

Native Olympia oysters are dwarfed by Pacific oyster. The larger bivalve was introduced after the diminutive native was almost eliminated from Northwest estuaries by overharvest and pollution.

Oyster growers in the Pacific Northwest were among the first to have grasped the economic threat of changing ocean conditions—particularly changes in ocean acidity. Though slight, the rise in acidity is projected to have a profound impact on larval oysters as they begin to form shells. Researchers have discovered that within the first 48 hours of life, oyster larvae must form shell structures in order to develop organs to feed themselves—the nutrients furnished within their eggs simply run out. During this time, shells are so fragile that minute changes in seawater acidity slow or prevent that growth, starving the larva before it can feed itself. The Pacific oyster may, in fact, be endangered, going the way of the native Olympia oyster it so effectively replaced in the Pacific Northwest estuary ecosystem.

pickleweed
Salicornia virginica

Estuaries are where saltwater and freshwater blend, creating challenges for all organisms that survive there. In seawater, salt and other minerals are concentrated at levels that are toxic to most organisms. Pickleweed is a terrestrial plant that breaks the rules. Like eelgrass, another true flowering plant, it has evolved to tolerate salt in order to exploit the rich nutrients available in estuary sediments.

The rule it breaks is a basic chemical process called osmosis, which says that water will flow through cell membranes toward solutions that are saltier. That's why the old remedy of soaking an infected finger in saltwater is supposed to work—it draws fluids out of a wound and promotes the circulation of healing blood to the infected area.

If all plants need water to survive, how does pickleweed absorb the freshwater it needs from saltwater? How does it store the salt within its tissues at levels that are safe for its plant tissues? Pickleweed absorbs its freshwater simply by being saltier inside—storing salt within its cells, so that the water it needs will flow spontaneously through its outer cell membranes. It stores its salt by diluting it to safe levels with freshwater stored in the plant in fleshy or "succulent" tissue—a characteristic shared with many cacti and other plants adapted to extreme dryness.

Look closely at the newest finger-like stems of pickleweed. They have a smooth, waxy, "pickley" surface. Break one open and notice the juicy, textured tissue inside. The final test is to pop some in your mouth. What do you notice? Yes! It has a crunchy texture and snappy, salty flavor. You aren't the only one who has noticed—it has become a favorite of many wild food foragers and chefs. ★

Getaway Guide

Take a weekend and add a day or two at either end and explore the Pacific Northwest Coast. The areas suggested below offer the best the coast has to offer, just hours away from our cities and suburbs and connected by highway and ferryboat. Each Getaway was selected because it offers a whole menu of natural history experience opportunities—you can visit each of the habitats in each locale. Grab your gear and go!

Botanical Beach, near Port Renfrew, boasts some of Vancouver Island's best tide pooling.

Vancouver Island Getaway

Experiencing nature on the shores of Vancouver Island can be as mild as walking the paths along Beacon Hill Park in Victoria or as wild as backpacking the wilderness of the West Coast Trail. Services for travelers are abundant and the locals are eager to show off the island's beauty and natural bounty.

Vancouver Island stretches nearly 300 miles from tip to tip, a barrier to the fierce lashings of storms off the not-so "Pacific" Ocean. Its southern tip is urban—half of the island's total population lives in the Victoria area. But as you venture north and west, Vancouver Island shows its wild sides. Scattered First Nations reserves and small coastal villages are set among vast tracts of forest and a welter of inlets and small islands. Just getting there entails twisting roads (watch for log trucks) or small, island-hopping ferries. Towering peaks rise as the island's backbone. Wildlife is abundant in the water, air, and on the land, so bring your binoculars.

Fortunately for the first-timer, or for the family intent on an introduction to exploring the coast, mild and wild are close at hand; your choices are many. The provincial capitol city of Victoria is a great first step. In addition to a taste of "Victorian" charm, the city is loaded with bike trails, waterfront parks, and promenades, as well as local whale-watching services, outdoor stores, bookstores, and everything you would need to wander farther afield and explore. The Royal British Columbia Museum is a great stop for an overview of British Columbia history and natural history.

Pacific Rim National Park Reserve

Pacific Rim National Park Reserve stretches along the island's wild, west coast. The park offers a variety of outstanding coastal adventures for first-timers and seasoned wilderness hikers and kayakers. In the front-country areas of the Long Beach Unit (located between the small towns of Ucluelet and Tofino), short hikes lead to coastal bogs, rainforests, and sand dunes. Explore miles of broad sand beaches or rocky coves and headlands that teem with tide-pool life. Gray whales migrate just offshore during spring.

The Pacific Rim Visitor Center is located on Highway 4, just as you approach the turn to Ucluelet. Passes and park information are available at the Park Administration office near Green Point Campground.

The small village of Ucluelet, east of the park, offers restaurants, hotels, and the Ucluelet Aquarium, built in 2012 and featuring live exhibits and education programs. A local loop trail, the Wild Pacific Trail, passes through dense coastal forest with vistas to beaches, the Pacific Ocean, and Barkley Sound.

Kwisitis Visitor Centre is an information station and base for guided interpretive walks that feature the rocky intertidal areas, sand beach, dunes, and the cultural traditions of the local Nuu-chah-nulth people. A restaurant, operated by local First Nations people, features a gourmet menu based on traditional foods. Nearby is the Shorepine Bog, with a fully accessible boardwalk trail loop.

Green Point is the park's campground area, midway between Ucluelet and Tofino. Campground tidiness is strictly enforced here—cougars, wolves, and bears move through the area frequently. Interpretive programs are offered at the indoor theater.

Long Beach is a world renowned surf spot, situated on a broad sand beach. Surfers and swimmers are warned about dangerous rip tides.

Tofino forms the western bookend community in the area. Surf shops, art galleries, stores, restaurants, and a variety of kayak and charter floatplane services are available.

End-to-end travel on Vancouver Island follows a route (Trans-Canada 1 from Victoria to Nanaimo and Highway 19 from Nanaimo to Port Hardy) along the

Long Beach in Pacific Rim National Park Reserve.

northeastern side of the island. To reach the Long Beach Unit of the park, leave Highway 19 near Parksville and drive over the island's crest to Port Alberni, located on a deep inlet, and then over Sutton Pass along Highway 4 to the coast itself. Distance between Victoria and Tofino is about 198 miles, or about five hours from Victoria.

Victoria, British Columbia, and the Gulf Islands

Victoria, British Columbia's provincial capitol, crowns the rocky southeast tip of Vancouver Island. Bustling with right-sized urbanity, its charm and intimate scale make it an exciting travel destination. The Royal British Columbia Provincial Museum is the ultimate visitor center. Exhibits on British Columbia's natural history and culture make you feel at home in the province. Whale-watching trips depart regularly out of the compact Inner Harbour area and the city's perimeter—saltwater all around—offers parks and beaches that invite bird watching and beachcombing within city limits. The ferry *Coho* makes regular trips to and from Port Angeles, the gateway to the Washington and the Olympic Peninsula, as well as to the United States.

Sidney

Located just minutes north of Victoria, on the Saanich Peninsula, Sidney is the western, and Canadian, end of the Washington State Ferries route through the San Juan Islands to Anacortes, Washington. It's appeal, however, goes beyond simply being a ferry terminal. The Shaw Ocean Discovery Centre, in downtown Sidney, is a compact, yet very informative aquarium and education facility dedicated to showing off the Salish Sea's dazzling array of sea creatures in a series of smart and sophisticated exhibits. Nearby is the ferry to Sidney Spit, a unit within Gulf Islands National Park Reserve, which provides access to its marshes and tide flats in summer.

Gulf Islands National Park Reserve

Accessible by ferry from Swartz Bay, Gulf Islands National Park Reserve is scattered across dozens of islands and includes marine areas between the islands. From here, you have access to Saltspring Island, with its arts, crafts, and food, and Mayne Island, Pender Islands, and Saturna Island, with their scattered units within the national park.

Tucked deep in Vancouver Island's "rain shadow," the Gulf Islands seem to fly off the eastern tip of the island toward their US counterparts, the San Juan Islands. Their unique place in southern Georgia Strait creates both remarkable marine and terrestrial habitats.

Things to do include shore-based whale watching (these are the home waters of the southern resident orcas), tide pooling, kayaking, hiking, birding, and studying unique plant communities.

Saturna Island, one of the "outer islands" and a close neighbor to the San Juans, offers the best and most diverse sampler of the biodiversity and scenic splendor of the Gulf Islands. About half of the island is within Gulf Islands National Park Reserve. Both compact and diverse, Saturna Island offers a wonderful introduction to this important Canadian treasure.

Winter Cove is a day use area, with picnic tables, restrooms, swimming, boat launching, and short hikes to view the Strait of Georgia and the turbulent Boat Passage. Mount Warburton Pike (1,303 feet) offers an invigorating hike, or a twisty drive to its summit. From there you are rewarded with spectacular views across the entire San Juan Islands archipelago. Narvaez Bay is at the southern tip of Saturna Island and represents the best of both marine and terrestrial habitats unique to the Gulf Islands. The pristine

Victoria, British Columbia, boasts urban amenities, provincial government and whale watching.

bay and native oak woodland and prairie are its principal attractions. Use caution when hiking on the rocky point. East Point is British Columbia's southernmost tip of land. Here you can view the lighthouse and possibly see orca whales from the shore. Swirling currents make this a very productive area for seabird watching. Other islands in the group are dotted with small communities interspersed with farms and vacation homes. Access is by small BC Ferries ferryboats that weave through the island passages. If you travel by BC Ferry between Swartz Bay and Tsawwassen, outside of Vancouver, pay close attention as the ship transits Active Pass between Mayne and Galiano Islands. Surging currents laden with plankton make this an important habitat for seabirds and marine mammals.

West of Victoria: Juan de Fuca Provincial Park

The coastline facing the Strait of Juan de Fuca offers a perfect introduction to Vancouver Island's shores. Miles of spectacular ocean views and hiking and exploring opportunities lie between Sooke and Port Renfrew, an inlet that forms a sharp notch in the coastline nearly opposite Cape Flattery, Washington's northwest tip.

An easy day or overnight trip from Victoria, Juan de Fuca Provincial Park lines the south-facing shore of the island. For serious backpackers, the Juan de Fuca Marine Trail threads a rugged coastal route along beaches and headlands. However, for the rest of us, access to some of its major features is easy, with relatively short hikes to the beach at developed sites, including China Beach, Sombrio Beach, and Botanical Beach. China Beach features a campground that is open seasonally. Trails lead through the forested uplands to the beaches. The eastern end of the Juan de Fuca Marine Trail is located at China Beach. Sombrio Beach is well known to Vancouver Island surfers. The beach is primarily cobble and features primitive campsites on the beach itself. The beach is reached by a ten-minute walk through coastal forest. There is also a spectacular waterfall, located in a narrow slot canyon east along the beach. Botanical Beach, in particular, is well worth the visit for its unusual geology and spectacular intertidal life. Pioneering marine biologist Josephine Tilden established a marine research station here between 1900 and 1907 and catalogued over 100 species of marine invertebrates. In order to protect the tide-pool communities, park staff enforce strict rules about removal or handling of marine animals.

Northern Salish Sea Getaway

Shared by Canada and the United States, northern Puget Sound and the southern Strait of Georgia form the northern end of the Salish Sea. The Salish Sea gets it name in honor of the Coastal Salish people, a large and geographically diverse linguistic grouping of individual tribes that inhabit the region. The name is loosely applied to all of Puget Sound and the Strait of Georgia. For our purposes, this "sea" is more accurately described as a complex of straits, passages, inlets and island archipelagoes that include Canada's Gulf Islands and the US San Juan Islands, and their surrounding and connecting waterways.

Because of their massive influxes of freshwater from numerous rivers, the Strait of Georgia and Puget Sound are technically part of a vast estuary system. Their combined scale, however, gives them the appearance of a large ocean inlet. We can consider them both—freshwater profoundly influences their oceanographic character; marine processes, like swells and waves, tides, upwelling, marine organisms, and food chains, give them their oceanic qualities.

Both British Columbia, in Canada, and Washington, in the United States, are gateways to the northern Salish Sea. Ferry routes connect the islands to the mainland in both countries and create the opportunity for an international experience that remains "local" for residents of the region. The diversity of habitats and activities involved in visiting them run the whole gamut of nature-appreciation experiences—forest hikes, tide pooling, whale watching, camping, bird watching, kayaking, and fishing—the list goes on.

Whidby and Fidalgo Islands and the Skagit Valley

The eastern shores of the Salish Sea are bounded by Whidby and Fidalgo Islands and the Skagit Valley, a broad agricultural delta created by the Skagit River carrying sediments from deep in the North Cascade Mountains. The Skagit River is known for large wintering populations of bald eagles that migrate from Alaska and Yukon Territory to feed on salmon runs. In the farmlands of the delta itself, large flocks of snow geese and trumpeter swans congregate through winter months.

Padilla Bay National Estuarine Research Reserve covers 11,000 acres of mudflat, and some of the largest eelgrass beds in the United States. The Breazeale Interpretive Center features exhibits on estuary habitats and wildlife. A variety of other estuary education programs are offered for youth and adults. Much of the estuary shoreline is accessible by trails and wildlife viewing is some of Washington's best. Nearby Bayview State Park offers camping. Deception Pass is a surging channel between Whidby and Fidalgo Islands spanned by a graceful bridge 180 feet above the water. Land on either side is within Deception Pass State Park. The park contains over 14 miles of saltwater shoreline and 38 miles of hiking trails along

A sea of islands connects the United States and Canada in the northern Salish Sea.

cliffs, in old-growth forest, and on dune-lined beaches. Rosario Beach, in the northern part of the park, is Puget Sound's most popular tide pooling area. Its position at the eastern end of the Strait of Juan de Fuca means that it is exposed to the full force of ocean swells that travel up the strait.

Anacortes and the San Juan Islands

From Washington, access to the San Juan Islands is by way of Washington State Ferries and the crossing between Anacortes and Sidney, British Columbia. Along the way, ferries stop at Lopez, Orcas, Shaw, and San Juan Islands. Access to other islands is strictly by private and commercial boats.

Anacortes is a bustling maritime community with a working waterfront that serves commercial fishing, recreational boating, shipbuilding, and, in the distance, moored tankers awaiting dock space at nearby oil refineries. Several commercial whale-watch services operate from here. Whale-watch boats range throughout the San Juans and Gulf Islands on four- to five-hour cruises searching for orcas, humpbacks, minke, and gray whales. About 2 miles west of Anacortes, near the Washington State Ferries terminal, Washington Park covers the tip of a peninsula jutting into the Salish Sea. The park's scenic-loop drive offers views and access to rocky shores and a small campground.

By ferry, the most popular island destinations are Lopez, Orcas, and San Juan Islands. Each offers a variety of natural environments and visitor amenities. Lopez Island is a popular cycling destination, known for its laid-back atmosphere and quiet country roads. Spencer Spit State Park is a popular campground and features beach and dune habitats. Shark Reef Sanctuary, a county park, is located at the southern end of the island and is known for its spectacular views, rocky intertidal habitat, and surging currents. Orcas Island, the San Juans' largest and highest, features Moran State Park, Washington's oldest state park, with its miles of densely forested trails and, at over 2,400 feet, Mount Constitution, with its commanding views. Eastsound is the principal business area with boutiques, restaurants, inns, and stores. Several whale-watch and kayak rental businesses are based on the island

San Juan Island, the second largest, is known for its bustling town of Friday Harbor, where the ferry

Ferryboat routes are the highways of the San Juan and Gulf Islands.

docks and orca whales are often spotted from viewpoints along the island's west side. Visit the Whale Museum and take advantage of local businesses offering whale-watching cruises, kayak tours and rentals, and a host of other visitor services. San Juan Island National Historical Park commemorates a near-war between the United States and England in 1859. The conflict, caused by a pig owned by an Irishman and killed for eating the potatoes of an American farmer, escalated because, at the time, the San Juan Islands were disputed territory between the nations. Fortunately, cooler heads prevailed, sorted out the border, settled the dispute and averted war.

Olympic Coast Getaway

Crowded between the vast Pacific Ocean and the lofty Olympic Mountains, the coast of the Olympic Peninsula is, by nature, wild to the extreme. Much of the coastal strip is protected as wilderness in Olympic National Park. And an area over 3,000 square miles of the marine environment is protected in Olympic Coast National Marine Sanctuary, to a distance of over 25 miles offshore. Nowhere in the lower 48 states can you experience so much undeveloped shoreline and the isolation and grandeur of a true wilderness coastline. However, this doesn't mean that the Olympic Coast is reserved only for backpacking adventurers. Along its length, there are trailheads, highway vistas, campgrounds, and beaches that require minimum effort in exchange for maximum enjoyment.

Cape Flattery, the northwesternmost point of the lower 48 states.

Port Angeles

Tucked in a large natural harbor, Port Angeles is a good jumping-off point for an Olympic Coast getaway. For visitors coming from Canada, it is their first step into the United States. There are things to do literally within minutes of clearing customs. The Arthur D. Feiro Marine Life Center, with its touch tanks and live exhibits, and NOAA's Olympic Coast Discovery Center, with interactive exhibits on ocean exploration and conservation, are right next door to the ferry terminal. Walk or bike along the Olympic Discovery Trail to stretch your legs and get views of the Strait of Juan de Fuca and, on clear days, distant Mount Baker. During summer months, whale-watch tours operate from the Port Angeles Boat Haven.

To the east, explore Dungeness Spit National Wildlife Refuge, a birding hotspot with quiet inner harbor and wave-beaten outer cobble beaches. To the south, stop at the Olympic National Park Visitor Center on your way to Hurricane Ridge, a mile above sea level, with sweeping views into the Olympic Mountains and north to Vancouver Island. To the west, start your Olympic Coast exploration with a stop at Tongue Point, in Salt Creek Recreation Area, a county park that boasts the finest tide pooling along the US side of the Strait of Juan de Fuca.

Neah Bay and La Push:
The Makah and Quileute Indian Reservations

Each its own sovereign nation, the Makah and Quileute Tribes are generous hosts in their territories. The villages of Neah Bay and La Push have been occupied for millennia by these Native Americans and their ancestors because of the abundance of marine and forest resources and the wealth it furnished. Today the communities are homes to tribal members as well as fishing ports for tribal, sport, and other commercial fishers. Each has stores, restaurants, resort cabins, and campgrounds for visitors.

In Neah Bay, make sure to set aside enough time to tour the Makah Museum and its collection of artifacts, many of which were excavated from a whaling village at Ozette, located farther south along the coast. The museum's gift store sells books and native artwork. The museum also offers interpretive programs led by Makah Tribe members at Cape Flattery, on the northwest tip of the Olympic Peninsula (and the lower 48 states). The half-mile hike to Cape Flattery is spectacular in itself, but very rewarding when seen through Makah eyes with the aid of the Makah naturalists. South of Neah Bay, the Shi Shi trailhead, located near the Makah National Fish Hatchery, provides access to Shi Shi beach and the northern end of Olympic National Park's coastal wilderness. The distance to the Olympic National Park boundary and the northern tip of Shi Shi is 2 miles. A Makah Recreation Permit is required for reservation visitors. Make sure to display it in your car windshield when parking at trailheads. Camping and cabins are available at the Makah Tribe's Hobuck Beach Resort.

The Makah Museum, in Neah Bay, houses thousands of objects linking the Makah people to the land and the sea.

At La Push, the broad sweep of First Beach looks out to James Island, a fortress of rock just across the mouth of the Quillayute River. Groceries, cabins, and camping are available at the Lonesome Creek Resort on the beach. The trailhead to Second Beach is located a short distance up the road from the First Beach. The trail crosses into Olympic National Park within its first several hundred yards, climbs gently, then drops to Second Beach in seven-tenths of a mile.

Makah and Quileute people are, by tradition, hospitable and welcoming in their homelands. It is important, however, to remember etiquette as a visitor:

- Please obey signs and posted tribal regulations.
- Respect the privacy of homes and private and tribal property.
- Don't assume you can photograph individuals or cultural activities. Ask first.
- Do not disturb or remove artifacts or natural objects.

Olympic National Park

Kalaloch, one of the few areas accessible by car on the rugged Olympic Coast.

Federal agencies protect about 65 miles of coastline, 48 of which are designated as wilderness. Road access to much of the Olympic Coast is limited. To the north, the Hoko Road leads to Lake Ozette, the trailhead to Cape Alava and Sand Point, each about a 3½ mile hike from the Ozette Ranger

Station and campground. State Route 110 and the Mora Road to Rialto Beach, west of the town of Forks. Take the Oil City Road to Oil City (sorry, no oil, no city; just a trailhead), near the mouth of the Hoh River. Highway 101 runs along the beach for several miles near Kalaloch.

There are campgrounds at Lake Ozette, Mora, and Kalaloch. Seasonal interpretive programs are offered at Mora and Kalaloch, including evening programs and guided beach walks. Inland, be sure not to miss the Hoh Rain Forest with its famed and often-photographed Hall of Mosses Trail. A visitor center and interpretive programs are provided at the Hoh Campground. For hikers, the Olympic Coast wilderness offers both easy and strenuous hikes, from casual day hikes of just a few miles, to expedition-quality multiday backpacking trips along this entire section of rugged coastline. Check the Olympic National Park website for hiking information or stop at any national park visitor center for more information.

Southern Beaches

South of Olympic National Park, the coastline of the Olympic Peninsula shifts in character, opening onto broad sand beaches, backed by low foothills and dotted with small beach communities. With the exception of

Broad sand beaches line the southern Washington coastline. Bluffs at Iron Springs glow in late light.

the Quinault Indian Reservation, whose beaches are closed to nontribal members due to vandalism and abuse in the 1960s, beaches are managed by Washington State Parks. Many sections of the beach are open to motor vehicles for part of the year. Here, beachcombing, razor clamming, and surf perch fishing are popular activities and contribute heavily to local economies. The communities of Moclips, Pacific Beach, Copalis, and Ocean Shores offer visitor amenities such as stores, motels, resorts, and campgrounds. Pacific Beach and Ocean City state parks have picnic areas, campsites, and ample beach access. Griffiths-Priday State Park is for day-use only, but features a long section of beach along the Copalis River spit.

For intrepid canoeists and kayakers, a short paddle up the Copalis River takes you to the Copalis Ghost Forest, an as-yet undeveloped site owned by Washington State Parks. Here are the silver skeletons of trees drowned when a massive earthquake shook the region in 1700, causing the land to be flooded when the ground dropped abruptly.

In Ocean Shores, visit the Ocean Shores Interpretive Center for exhibits on local natural history. In April and May, visit Grays Harbor National Wildlife Refuge, in Hoquiam, to observe thousands of migrating shorebirds. The Grays Harbor Shorebird Festival takes place each year around the end of April.

Lewis and Clark Getaway

Where the West's greatest river joins the world's largest ocean, human history and nature come crashing together with the force of swells breaking at the foot of Cape Disappointment. For millennia, this was the meeting place of river Native Americans with coastal Native Americans and the intersection of a trade network stretching well beyond the Rockies and far north and south along the Pacific Northwest Coast.

It was curiosity, the beaver, and visions of empire that brought Lewis and Clark, and, after that, trappers and traders. Thomas Jefferson's instructions were mainly borne of his own insatiable appetite for natural history and geography, coupled with the need to appraise a piece of new property the United States had recently bought from France—the Louisiana Purchase.

It was here that Lewis and Clark's Corps of Discovery reached the Pacific, wintering into 1806 among Chinook and Clatsop Indians and recording every minute detail of natural phenomena they encountered. Feel like exploring?

The Long Beach Peninsula

The longtime claim of the "world's longest beach" is difficult to prove. So let's just say this *is* a long beach. The Long Beach Peninsula juts due north from the hills bordering the Columbia River as a long expanse of sand beach, backed by dunes, coastal lakes, bogs and wetlands, and mixed shore pine and Sitka spruce forests. To the east is the vast estuary of Willapa Bay (known first as Shoalwater Bay, due to it's shallow depths—promoters of maritime shipping changed that!). Like many coastal beach areas, it is developed with homes and businesses catering to beachgoers. But wait—that attraction has a lot to do with the rich coastal ecosystem surrounding the developed parts of the peninsula. Throngs arrive each year to hunt for razor clams and to surf fish. Remnant dunes, forests, wetlands, and mudflats teem with birds in all seasons, making it one of the coast's great birding hotspots. And significant areas are set aside for hiking and nature watching and habitat protection in Willapa National Wildlife Refuge, Leadbetter State Park, and the Washington Coastal Conservation Area. The very tip of Leadbetter Point is an active restoration area for Snowy Plover and Oregon Silverspot Butterfly, imperiled throughout their ranges by human encroachment on their rare habitats.

Thomas Jefferson's curiosity brought Lewis and Clark across the West to study the geography of the Rocky Mountains and Pacific Northwest.

The Mouth of the Columbia

The Columbia's mouth, the famed and dreaded "Graveyard of the Pacific," divides the coast between Washington and Oregon. But the connection of the Astoria-Megler Bridge and Highway 101 links both sides of the river and creates a seamless opportunity to study history and nature in this natural ecosystem hotspot. Historically, the United States' territorial claim to much of the Pacific Northwest rested with the American Robert Gray's successful entry into the Columbia River in 1792. Lewis and Clark's occupation in 1805 and 1806 after traveling overland to reach the place helped seal the deal, as did John Jacob Astor's fur enterprise that came shortly after.

Aside from the spectacle of the Columbia River surging into the Pacific, the area abounds in natural wonders. And the complex of parks and protected areas that surrounds the river mouth provides great camping and much to explore. On the Washington side, visit Cape Disappointment State Park and the Lewis and Clark Interpretive Center. Hiking trails follow the Lewis and Clark route northward toward Long Beach. During summer, look for sooty shearwaters, ordinarily found farther out in the Pacific, near North Head Lighthouse. At Cape Disappointment, hike the forest trails,

Oregon and Washington are linked at Astoria, Oregon, just as the Northwest is linked to the Pacific Rim by maritime commerce.

explore pocket beaches, and look for nesting habitat for three species of cormorant: brant's, double-crested, and pelagic.

Lewis and Clark eventually settled on a winter camp on the river's south side because of the abundance of wildlife found on the Clatsop Plains. Lewis and Clark National and State Historical Park is comprised of Fort Stevens State Park and the newer interpretive center and reconstruction of Fort Clatsop. Summer interpretive reenactments bring the explorers' winter on the Oregon coast to life. Fort Stevens State Park is laced with a network of roads and trails that take you to a wide variety of coastal features, from broad beaches, to expanses of grassy dunes, to the rock-lined jetty at river's mouth, to coastal Sitka spruce and shore pine forests. History buffs will enjoy the old artillery emplacements and the rusting bones of the shipwreck *Peter Iredale*. Nearby towns of Astoria, Hammond, and Warrenton are well stocked with motels, restaurants, grocery stores, brew-pubs, and other attractions.

Overlooking the "Graveyard of the Pacific," Cape Disappointment stands witness to the violent meeting of the West's greatest river and Earth's largest ocean.

A beach playground for generations, Cannon Beach is, for many, an introduction to the marine environment.

Oregon's Famed Beaches

Lewis and Clark's natural history adventures led them south to what is now Seaside, where they evaporated salt from seawater. At Cannon Beach, they observed a beached whale. Today, Seaside, Gearhart, and Cannon Beach are renowned as some of Oregon's premier beach destinations. An easy drive from the Portland area, they attract hordes of visitors and can be very crowded during summer. However, interspersed among them are opportunities for hiking, beachcombing, and exploration where you can experience a less crowded feel. The rocky headland of Tillamook Head is accessible by winding trail through dense a Sitka spruce forest. The northern end of the trail is located just outside Seaside.

The southern terminus is Ecola State Park. Offshore, look for Tillamook Rock, with its famous lighthouse, "Terrible Tilly." The structure shares the lonely rock with thousands of seabirds. The viewpoint at Ecola State Park features sweeping scenic vistas along the coast, as well as lookouts for migrating gray whales. Pocket beaches, accessible by trail or at low tides, are far less crowded than the destination hot spots, and offer good tide pooling and wildlife watching.

Cannon Beach, with its famous 235-foot landmark, Haystack Rock, attracts large crowds and yet offers good beginner-level tide pooling and seabird watching (look for tufted puffins and pelagic cormorants). The area within 1,000 feet of Haystack Rock is dedicated as a conservation area, so disturbing intertidal life and climbing above the barnacle line are prohibited. Summer interpretive programs are offered by Friends of Haystack Rock, a nonprofit organization. Program schedules can be obtained at the local visitor center.

Capes and Coves Getaway

South of Cannon Beach, Highway 101 begins to wind between high exposed vistas of the ocean and inland, around sheltered bays and estuaries and lush farmland. This 100-mile stretch of Oregon's coast between Cannon Beach and Newport alternates between long sand beaches and headlands that jut into the Pacific and offer commanding views of the ocean, seabird

Vantage points like Cape Meares provide vistas for migrating whales and flocks of breeding seabirds.

colonies, and, in season, passing whales. Most of these headlands are the remnants of ancient lava flows that descended the ancient Columbia River from volcanic vents in what is now northeast Oregon and spread along the coastline.

Coast Range rivers, like the Nehalem, Nestucca, Wilson, Salmon, Siletz, and Yaquina Rivers, meet the sea in estuaries that teem with waterfowl and shorebirds, seals, and sea lions. Scattered rocky outcrops in coves, along beaches, and at the bases of headlands are crowded with intertidal life. Dune-covered sand spits and deep coastal forests provide hiking opportunities year-round.

Cape Falcon is located within Oswald West State Park. Named for a beloved, conservationist governor, the park wraps around Cape Falcon and Neahkahnie Mountain. Short Sands Beach, affectionately called "Short-ies" by surfers, is an easy stroll from the highway. Both north and south ends of the beach are good for tide pooling.

The Three Capes Loop Highway is a good scenic alternative to Highway 101 and provides access to communities and natural features along the coast. Cape Meares was named for British explorer John Meares. A short hike to the lighthouse provides sweeping views south to Three Arch Rocks National Wildlife Refuge, the breeding habitat for over 100,000 common murres—the largest south of Alaska. Look for large flocks feeding in the nearshore waters.

Cape Lookout forms a high, spruce-forested ridge jutting over 2 miles into the ocean. From a vantage point 600 feet over the waves, look for migrating gray whales from March to May. The high viewing angle lets you see the animals not just when they blow, but when they swim just below the water's surface.

Cape Kiwanda, near Pacific City, is separated from the mainland by a dune field that attracts hang gliders. Unlike neighboring capes, Kiwanda is composed of yellowish, fossil-bearing sandstones—marine sedimentary rocks containing evidence of the early evolution of marine mammals. Short trails lead to viewpoints that overlook Oregon's "other" Haystack Rock. To the south, the Nestucca Spit is accessible through Bob Straub State Park. Broad beaches, dunes, and shorepine forests line the spit.

Cascade Head is a high ridge overlooking the Salmon River estuary. Parts of the area are managed by the Nature Conservancy. Other sections are part of Siuslaw National Forest. Protected as critical habitat for endemic plants and Oregon silverspot butterfly, access to portions of the high, open, meadowed headland is limited seasonally. Look for native grasses and the rare hairy checkermallow, Cascade Head catchfly, and early blue violet. An inland trail winds through a majestic coastal Sitka spruce and western hemlock forest with spruce trees reaching 6 feet in diameter.

Yaquina Head is the region's most popular tide pooling area, offering spectacular intertidal exploring, along with a visitor center and guided naturalist activities. Because its popularity and a long history of trampling, mussel beds are marked off-limits. Nevertheless, on a good low tide, lots of pools and rocky areas are open for exploration. The viewpoint at the lighthouse is a good spot for seeing migrating gray whales and flocks of common murres.

Oregon Dunes Getaway

Oregon's coastal dunes stretch nearly 50 miles along the coast, making it the largest coastal dunescape in the country. Dunes line the beaches and spits and, in places, extend miles inland as landscapes of stark sea swells of sand interspersed with forest islands, bogs, lakes, and streams. These eerie landscapes are constantly in motion as billions of wind-blown sand grains that originated on the seafloor advance landward, encroaching on forests, roads, wetlands, and developed areas.

Coastal forests show a different character through this region. Although Sitka spruce, western red cedar, and western hemlock are common in moister areas, shore pine becomes prevalent, especially along dune-field edges. The drier soils also support evergreen huckleberry and Pacific rhododendron. Darlingtonia Wayside, a state natural area just north of Florence, contains a magnificent bog packed with *Darlingtonia*, a carnivorous pitcher plant.

Although dunes exist, on a smaller scale, as far north as Vancouver Island and south into California, the area between the Siuslaw River mouth, near Florence, and Coos Bay, include the best examples of living dune systems and their associated lakes, streams, and grass and forest communities. Both within and outside of pubic parklands, large tracts of dunes are used by off-road vehicles. However, many areas remain off-limits to motorized recreation. Where off-road vehicles are allowed, dune buggy rentals and tours are offered by commercial operators.

Jessie M. Honeyman Memorial State Park is Oregon's most popular dune state park and is a good family destination and introduction to sand dunes. In addition to dune exploration, it offers Cleawox Lake, with a swimming area and a very kid-friendly campground.

Oregon Dunes National Recreation Area, managed by the US Forest Service, is spread along the coast between the Siuslaw River, at Florence, and the Coos River, near Coos Bay. The area is bisected by the Umpqua River estuary, near Reedsport, where the area headquarters and visitor center are located. Within the recreation area, there are many campgrounds, day-use areas, viewpoints, trails, boardwalks, and off-road vehicle areas that make dune exploration accessible to everyone.

The sea delivers the sand and the wind carries it over miles of shifting terrain.

Inland (east of Highway 101), lies a string of forested lakes with opportunities for hiking, boating, camping, and fishing. Follow signs to campgrounds and access points for Woahink, Siltcoos, Tahkenitch, Clear, and Tenmile Lakes.

Follow Highway 38 along the Umpqua River east from Reedsport about 3 miles to the Dean Creek Elk Viewing Area. A herd of 100 elk remain in the vicinity year-round. Parking and viewing platforms provide easy access, yet maintain a safe (for them and you) distance from the animals.

Nearby, visit South Slough National Estuarine Research Reserve and Cape Arago State Park, outside of Charleston, Oregon. South Slough is an excellent example of a coastal estuary system with its surrounding forest. A visitor center provides information on the estuary and is the trailhead for several forest hikes leading to the estuary and its associated marshes. Cape Arago State Park features seal and sea lion haul-outs and excellent tide pooling.

Redwood Highway Getaway

The fog-shrouded redwood forests of Del Norte and Humboldt counties in northern California are true wonders of the world. After a bitter contest between the timber industry and conservationists through much of the twentieth century, important fragments of this rare community survived. Although Pacific redwood forests occur to the south along the California coast, other forest community associations (such as Roosevelt elk and Sitka spruce) and neighboring ocean conditions allow us to claim the northernmost redwood groves as part of the Pacific Northwest. Similarly, the small tourist, timber, and fishing towns are difficult to tell apart from their Oregon, Washington, and coastal British Columbia counterparts.

A "Redwood Highway" vacation stretches beyond a typical weekend if you live in the metro areas of the I-5 corridor. However, a getaway to the redwoods, with its mix of coastal forest and beach explorations, will stretch your naturalist knowledge with its similarities and differences compared to other Pacific Northwest nature experiences.

The centerpiece of the experience lies in Redwood State and National Parks, a unique collection of redwood groves preserved in a unique partnership between the National Park Service and California State Parks. Around the edges are the Klamath and Smith River estuaries, the Tolowa Dunes, and a coastal strip of lagoons, marshes, and secluded beaches.

Naturally, the principal attractions are the redwoods themselves. Massive groves in Jedediah Smith Redwoods, Del Norte Coast Redwoods, and Prairie Creek Redwoods State Parks are connected by additions made in the 1960s and 70s. In 1978, Congress added land in the Redwood Creek watershed, expanding Redwood National Park dramatically and protecting

The legacy of conservation is memorialized in the living giants of the redwood forest.

not just the trees, but a watershed system threatened with siltation and flooding—twin results of logging and road building.

Park visitor centers in Crescent City and in Prairie Creek and Jedediah Smith Redwoods State Parks, and the Redwood Information Center, near Orick, are good places to get oriented to the combined parks. Evening programs and walks guided by park interpreters are informative and easy ways to get to know the area. Drop into a visitor center, attend a few programs, and then set out on your own for a memorable redwoods adventure.

Named groves are located in each of the park units and a visit to any of them is awe-inspiring. Quietly roam the Stout and Simpson-Reed Groves in Jedediah Smith Redwoods State Park, the Big Tree Wayside in Prairie Creek Redwoods State Park, and the Lady Bird Johnson Grove in adjacent Redwood National Park. For a strenuous hike from ridge top to river bottom, hike to the Tall Trees Grove. Access off the Bald Hills Road is limited, but free permits are available at the Redwood Information Center.

The hike to Enderts Beach is a good warm-up for exploring its tide pool.

For contrast from the big trees, visit Tolowa Dunes State Park and Lake Earl Wildlife Area, located north of Crescent City. Here, forests, marshes,

grasslands dunes, and open lagoon areas lie just inland from the coast. Lakes Earl and Tolowa are actually coastal lagoons that, in presettlement times, occasionally opened to the sea. This is considered one of the best birding areas in redwood country.

Gold Bluffs and Fern Canyon are located along the coast within Prairie Creek Redwoods State Park. Ochre-colored bluffs tower above low vegetated dunes and stunted clusters of trees. Elk are often seen in the dunes and along the road at the foot of the bluffs. The short hike into Fern Canyon is like stepping into the movie *Jurrasic Park*. In fact, scenes were filmed in the verdant, winding canyon, named for its dewy maidenhair ferns. Elk Meadows, also in Prairie Creek Redwoods State Park, is named for a large herd of Roosevelt elk that frequent the open area near the campground and neighboring lands outside the park. Mornings and evenings are the best time to observe the herd.

Enderts Beach, just south of the coastal plain that surrounds Crescent City, lies at the northern end of a steep headland. To visit the beach, follow Enderts Beach Road to the parking lot at its end, then continue along the trail high above the beach. Coastal bluff plants abound, along with views that, during gray whale migration season, should yield whale sightings. Drop off the trail to Enderts Beach for excellent tide pooling and beachcombing. The coastal trail continues beyond the beach along an old highway bed, winding deep into a magnificent redwood forest.

Numerous county and state park campgrounds are outside the state and national park complex, along with other visitor attractions. In addition to park headquarters, Crescent City offers many visitor amenities—motels, grocery stores, restaurants, and gas stations.

Safety and Equipment

Planning and preparation precede doing—or, at least they should. Stepping outside is always a step into the environment and its changing conditions. Take weather, for example: rain or shine? Check the forecast or take a look out the window, and attempt to dress appropriately. That's a simple one. But a trip to the coast involves many variables beyond just weather. What's the terrain like? Is it muddy, rocky, sandy, slippery? Will it be windy? Will it be foggy or clear, hot or cold? Because this is the Pacific Northwest, it could be all of those things—often on the same day. Being prepared is the best way to be safe and comfortable.

Safety First

It's a jungle out there. Every year, unwise or unprepared people run into trouble in the woods or on the beach. Usually, the consequences are just a sobering lesson. Sometimes, though, they are serious and even tragic. Most accidents arise from a lack of situational awareness—translated, that means paying attention to conditions and your surroundings. In the wild places we visit, nature's forces far exceed our own. The ocean, rivers, steep terrain, and weather can catch us by surprise if we aren't paying attention.

No matter where you're headed, the following are some basic safety guidelines that should be followed:

BE PREPARED Know the area and its hazards and be properly equipped for conditions. Get local information.

STAY ALERT Situations can change quickly; daylight, weather, and tides are dynamic.

DON'T OVERESTIMATE YOURSELF Sun, heat, thirst, and fatigue can compromise your judgment and abilities.

TAKE A PARTNER Solitude is nice, but the buddy system is better.

KEEP AN EYE ON KIDS Young adventurers are often too adventurous. Steep bluffs, rip tides, and river currents are very dangerous for children, so keep a close eye on them.

Hiking Safety

- Carry essential gear
- Sign the trail register or let someone know where you will be
- Be careful at stream crossings
- Keep your party together

Tide Pooling Safety

- Always keep an eye on incoming waves
- Know the tides in your location
- Watch your surroundings for signs of incoming tides
- Don't get stranded beneath cliffs or on rocks or islands
- Use a headlamp or lantern after dark
- Use a walking stick
- Avoid stepping on slippery seaweed
- Don't climb on rocks or bluffs

Wildlife-Watching Safety

- Don't get too close to seals and sea lions on the beach
- Don't attempt to "rescue" animals
- Keep pets under control and on a leash at all times
- Report aggressive wildlife or animals acting strangely
- Don't feed animals
- Don't approach animals to observe or get a picture; maintain your distance with a spotting scope or telephoto lens

Whale-Watching Safety

- Always follow crew instructions
- Hold on to railings—remember, "one hand for the boat"
- Drink water; sun and sea can dry you out
- Remember safety procedures (pay attention to the captain's briefings at the start)
- Watch your step on stairs, ladders, and in doorways

Photography Safety

- Use your optics (lenses) to get close to wildlife, and not your body

- Don't get "lost in the picture"; stay focused on reality (that wave or cliff), as well as your subject

- A waterproof camera will let you pay attention to your own safety, as opposed to the camera's

Recommended Equipment

As a fashion, technical outdoor clothing is as "Pacific Northwest" as the rain itself. That's not a coincidence. Pacific Northwesters spend a lot of time outdoors, rain or shine, and it's comfort that we seek under all conditions. Having the right gear means we can enjoy nature on its own terms. Being borderline hypothermic is no way to appreciate our natural surroundings.

Proper equipment is the next step to being prepared. Good binoculars, field guides, snacks, and other items, depending on your destination, will make your trip more worthwhile—you'll see more and learn more.

Here are some of the basics that you should carry with you on any outdoor excursion:

DAYPACK

SUNSCREEN AND SUNGLASSES

HAT

NONCOTTON LAYERS (base layer, insulation, shell)

APPROPRIATE FOOTWEAR

WATER

POCKET KNIFE

SNACKS

CELL PHONE (in a protective case, of course)

BINOCULARS

CAMERA

FIELD GUIDES

TOILET PAPER IN A ZIPLOCK BAG

ROAD MAP OR REGIONAL GUIDE

Hiking Equipment

- ☐ boots or low-cut hikers
- ☐ map and compass
- ☐ trekking poles
- ☐ extra snacks
- ☐ small first-aid kit
- ☐ headlamp

Tide Pooling Equipment

- ☐ waterproof or "self-draining" footwear
- ☐ water-resistant camera
- ☐ wading staff (like an old ski pole—not your pricey trekking poles)
- ☐ magnifying glass
- ☐ intertidal identification guide
- ☐ zip-offs (convertible pants) or beach shorts
- ☐ notebook and pen
- ☐ small shovel or trowel
- ☐ tide tables

Wildlife-Watching Equipment

- ☐ spotting scope and tripod
- ☐ camera with telephoto lens
- ☐ plant, bird, and wildlife field guides
- ☐ extra layers (for sitting still)
- ☐ notebook and pen

Whale-Watching Equipment

- ☐ nonslip footwear
- ☐ heavy raingear
- ☐ motion-sickness medication
- ☐ marine wildlife field guides
- ☐ cash (for snacks and tips for crew)
- ☐ camera with telephoto lens
- ☐ warming gloves or hand warmers

Photography Equipment

- ☐ protective camera bag and rain cover
- ☐ camera
- ☐ tripod
- ☐ extra lenses
- ☐ polarizing filter
- ☐ pack towel and lens cloths
- ☐ fingerless gloves
- ☐ notebook and pen
- ☐ spare batteries and memory cards
- ☐ plastic bags to protect sensitive equipment from moisture

References

Carefoot, T. 1977. *Pacific Seashores: A Guide to Intertidal Ecology*. Seattle: University of Washington Press.

Davis, L. D. 2009. *The Northwest Nature Guide*. Portland, Oregon: Timber Press.

Denny, M. W., and S. D. Gaines, eds. 2007. *Encyclopedia of Tidepools and Rocky Shores*. Berkeley: University of California Press.

Dombrowski, T. 2014. *Seaside Walks on Vancouver Island*. Victoria, British Columbia: Rocky Mountain Books.

Dunegan, L. 2009. *Insider's Guide to the Oregon Coast*. 4th ed. Guilford, Connecticut: Globe Pequot Press.

Evarts, J., and M. Popper, eds. 2001. *Coast Redwood: A Natural and Cultural History*. Los Olivos, California: Cachuma Press.

Groot, C., and L. Margolis, eds. 1991. *Pacific Salmon Life Histories*. Vancouver: University of British Columbia Press.

Harbo, R. 1980. *Tidepool and Reef*. Surrey, British Columbia, and Blaine, Washington: Harbour House Publishers.

———. 1999. *Whales to Whelks: Coastal Marine Life of Oregon, Washington, British Columbia and Alaska*. Madeira Park, British Columbia: Harbour Publishing.

———. 2010. *A Field Guide to Nudibranchs of the Pacific Northwest*. Madeira Park, British Columbia: Harbour Publishing.

Hickey, B. M., and N. S. Banas. 2003. "Oceanography of the U.S. Pacific Northwest Coastal Ocean and Estuaries with Application to Coastal Ecology." *Estuaries* 26 (4B): 1010–1031.

Kauffman, M. E. 2013. *Conifers of the Pacific Slope: a Field Guide to the Conifers of California, Oregon, and Washington*. Kneeland, California: Backcountry Press.

Kozloff, E. N. 1983. *Seashore Life of the Northern Pacific Coast: an Illustrated Guide to Northern California, Oregon, Washington, and British Columbia*. Seattle: University of Washington Press.

Mass, C. 2008. *The Weather of the Pacific Northwest*. Seattle: University of Washington Press.

McPhee, M. 1987. *Western Oregon: Portrait of the Land and its People*. Helena, Montana: American Geographic Publishing.

Morse, R. W. 2001. *A Birder's Guide to Coastal Washington*. Olympia, Washington: R.W. Morse Co.

Niesen, T. M. 1982. *The Marine Biology Coloring Book*. New York: Barnes and Noble Books.

———. 1997. *Beachcomber's Guide to Marine Life of the Pacific Northwest*. Houston, Texas: Gulf Publishing Co.

O'Brien, M., R. Crossley, and K. Karlson. 2006. *The Shorebird Guide*. Boston, Massachusetts: Houghton Mifflin Co.

Ricketts, E. F., and J. Calvin. 1968. *Between Pacific Tides*. 4th ed. Stanford, California: Stanford University Press.

Schultz, S. T. 1990. *The Northwest Coast: a Natural History*. Portland, Oregon: Timber Press.

Sibley, D. A. 2001. *The Sibley Guide to Bird Life and Behavior*. New York: Knopf.

———. 2003. *The Sibley Field Guide to Birds of Western North America*. New York: Knopf.

Steelquist, R. U. 1985. *Olympic National Park and the Olympic Peninsula: A Traveler's Companion*. Del Mar, California: Woodlands Press.

———. 1987. *Washington's Coast*. Helena, Montana: American Geographic Publishing.

———. 1989. *Ferryboat Field Guide to Puget Sound*. Helena, Montana: American Geographic Publishing.

———. 1992. *Field Guide to the Pacific Salmon*. Seattle, Washington: Sasquatch Books.

Sullivan, W. L. 2014. *100 Hikes/Travel Guide: Oregon Coast and Coast Range*. 3rd ed. Eugene, Oregon: Navillus Press.

Swanson, S., and M. Smith. 2013. *Must-See Birds of the Pacific Northwest*. Portland, Oregon: Timber Press.

Weideman, A. M. 1984. *The Ecology of Pacific Northwest Coastal Sand Dunes: A Community Profile*. US Fish and Wildlife Service FWS/OBS-84/04.

Weinmann, F., et al. 1984. *Wetland Plants of the Pacific Northwest*. Seattle, Washington: Seattle District, US Army Corps of Engineers.

Werthhiem, A. 1984. *The Intertidal Wilderness*. San Francisco, California: Sierra Club Books.

Windh, J. 2010. *The Wild Side Guide to Vancouver Island's Pacific Rim*. 2nd ed. Madeira Park, British Columbia: Harbour Publishing.

Online Resources

Government

British Columbia Provincial Parks
env.gov.bc.ca/bcparks/
California State Parks
parks.ca.gov
National Park Service
nps.gov
NOAA Olympic Coast National Marine Sanctuary
olympiccoast.noaa.gov
Oregon State Parks
oregonstateparks.org
Parks Canada
pc.gc.ca
US Forest Service
fs.fed.us
Washington State Parks
parks.wa.gov

General Information

The Cornell Lab of Ornithology
birds.cornell.edu

Conservation

National Audubon Society
audubon.org
The Nature Conservancy
nature.org
Ocean Futures Society
oceanfutures.org
Oceana
usa.oceana.org
Surfrider Foundation
surfrider.org
Sylvia Earle Alliance, Mission Blue
mission-blue.org

Photo Credits

All photographs by the author, except for the following:

Index

About the Author

Robert Steelquist is a native Pacific Northwest writer, photographer, naturalist, and environmental educator. Over his 30-year career, he has introduced readers, audiences, and students to nature in the Northwest through books, lectures, nature walks, backpacking trips, river floats, teacher workshops, and other outdoor learning adventures.